PAINLESS

English for Speakers of Other Languages

PAINLESS English for Speakers of Other Languages

Jeffrey Strausser
José Paniza

BARRON'S

All inquiries should be addressed to:
Barron's Educational Series, Inc.
250 Wireless Boulevard
Hauppauge, New York 11788
www.barronseduc.com

ISBN-13: 978-0-7641-3562-0
ISBN-10: 0-7641-3562-7

Library of Congress Catalog No.: 2006018471

Library of Congress Cataloging-in-Publication Data

Strausser, Jeffrey.
Painless English for speakers of other languages / Jeffrey Strausser, José Paniza.
p. cm.
ISBN-13: 978-0-7641-3562-0
ISBN-10: 0-7641-3562-7
1. English language—Study and teaching—Foreign speakers. 2. Middle school students—Language. 3. English language—Textbooks for foreign speakers. I. Paniza, José. II. Title.

PE1128.S885 2007
428.0071—dc22 2006018471

PRINTED IN CANADA
9 8 7 6 5 4 3 2

Dedication

This book is dedicated to my wife, Beth, and my children, Katie and Matt. Thank you for being my inspiration and motivation. May you never stop learning.

Jeff

This book is dedicated with love to my wife, Betty Jo, and my daughters, Jennifer and Lauren.

José

CONTENTS

Introduction: What This Book Will Do for You

Learning a new language is a lifetime challenge that can be lots of fun, but sometimes it can be very frustrating. Many times, your school textbook doesn't help you because it assumes you are already familiar with all the basics of the English language. The good news is this book can help. It starts from the beginning with *parts of speech* and then moves on to *spelling*, *vocabulary*, and *punctuation*. Once you have firmly established this foundation, you will be ready to write *sentences*, and later, *essays* and *stories*. Every section has lots of examples and an exercise group to help make sure that you understand the material. In addition, nearly 75 percent of the 62 sets of exercises have a theme associated with Social Studies or Science, so at the same time you are learning English, you are also learning Social Studies or Science. It's easy to find the areas you have questions about because all the basics are right here in this book. Finally, for the **Internet** surfers, each chapter contains web addresses where you can surf to read additional information about the topics discussed. It is not necessary to refer to these sites, as each section is concisely but thoroughly explained within the pages of the chapter. Nonetheless, if surfing through the ocean of cyberspace is fun for you, just look for the ***Surf's Up!*** box and check out the web pages listed there.

Do you want to improve how you speak and write in English? If so, start in wherever you feel comfortable. Everything is here waiting for you. You'll discover just how ***painless*** it is to improve your English skills!

Web Addresses Change!

You should be aware that addresses on the World Wide Web are constantly changing. Although every attempt has been made to provide you with the most current addresses available, the nature of the Internet makes it virtually impossible to keep abreast of the many changes that seem to occur on a daily basis.

If you should come across a web address (URL) that no longer appears to be valid, either because the site not longer exists or because the address has changed, don't panic. Simply do a **key word search** on the subject matter in question. For example, if you are interested in finding out more about compound-complex sentences and the particular address appears to be invalid, do a search for various words related to **compound-complex sentences**. These are the key words. A key word search might include, for example, **sentence types**. If an initial key word search provides too many potential sites, you can always narrow the number of choices by doing a second key word search that will limit your original search to only those sites that contain the terms from both your first and second searches.

WARNING: Not every response to your search will match your criteria, and some sites may contain adult material. If you are ever in doubt, check with a parent, teacher, or librarian who can help you.

PART ONE

Parts of Speech

CHAPTER ONE

Nouns

The English language divides words into eight *parts of speech*: nouns, pronouns, verbs, adjectives, adverbs, prepositions, conjunctions, and interjections. These parts of speech are the "building blocks" of good English. All of these building blocks are necessary for you to understand so that you can better speak and write English. Let's start out with one of the most important parts of speech—the ***noun***.

WHAT IS A NOUN?

Nouns are important because without them you wouldn't be able to name anything. You wouldn't have a name, and neither would your friends! Thankfully, you have nouns. A *noun* is a part of speech that names

- A person
- A place
- A thing
- An idea
- An animal
- A quality
- An activity

Below are some examples of nouns. Notice their variety.

> *Juan* is reading. (a person)
> *Dallas* is north of *Houston*. (a place, a place)
> The *rock* is very heavy. (a thing)
> *Philosophy* is very interesting. (an idea)
> My *cat* is chasing the *mouse*. (an animal, an animal)
> Overcoming *fear* requires great *courage*. (a quality, a quality)

Finally, we have:

> *Writing* is important. (an activity)

This last example is a little confusing. *Writing* is a noun because it names an activity; it isn't *performing* the activity, which is what a verb does. By contrast, notice how *writing* is used in the following sentence:

> Roberto is *writing* his name.

Here, *writing* is a verb, rather than a noun because it is the *action* Robert is performing.

This variety makes the noun important in the English language. We can name so many things! Before we go on, try the following exercises. They will give you a chance to identify the different types of **nouns** and what they name.

BRAIN TICKLERS!
Set #1
READING AND WRITING IN ENGLISH

Identify the ***nouns*** in each of the sentences below and underline them.

EXAMPLE:

My name is Elissa.

1. Ms. Garcia is my language arts teacher.
2. She has lived in the United States for ten years.
3. Reading is an important skill to learn.
4. We read stories from all over the world.
5. Besides being a good reader, I also want to be able to write English well.
6. I think reading stories will help me to learn to write English.
7. Reading and writing English well will take time and hard work.
8. I spend time every day learning new words and using the new words in sentences.
9. I write my words and sentences in my notebook.
10. Last week, I wrote a story in my notebook and then typed it on the computer.

(Answers are on page 247.)

As you can see, there are a great many nouns. You can learn about nouns more easily by dividing them into groups and learning about those groups. Let's begin by grouping nouns into ***proper nouns*** and ***common nouns***.

PROPER AND COMMON NOUNS

Most nouns are ***common nouns.*** A common noun names *any* person, place, thing, idea, animal, quality, or action. By contrast, a ***proper noun*** names a *specific* person, place, thing, idea, animal, quality, or action. It's important to learn the difference because proper nouns must be CAPITALIZED. Below are some examples of ***common nouns*** and ***proper nouns***.

Common Noun	Proper Noun
girl	Rosa
city	Chicago
holiday	Christmas
month	January
country	United States
building	Capitol

As you can see, common nouns name people *(girl)*, places *(country)*, and things (*building*) generally. By comparison, proper nouns name ***specific*** people (*Rosa*), places (*United States*), and things (*Capitol*). The following exercise will give you a chance to pick out ***common nouns*** and ***proper nouns***.

BRAIN TICKLERS!
Set #2
THE BRITISH COLONIES IN 18TH-CENTURY AMERICA

Single underline the ***common nouns*** and double underline the ***proper nouns*** in the sentences below.

EXAMPLE:

By 1750, Great Britain controlled a large area of North America.

The British controlled the land from what is now Maine to the northern border of Florida.

1. This land was home to nearly one million Europeans.
2. A quarter million Africans and a quarter million Native Americans also lived there.
3. Historians divide this area into three regions.
4. Massachusetts, Connecticut, Rhode Island, and New Hampshire comprised the colonies of New England.
5. Fishing became an important source of money for small towns along the Atlantic Ocean.

6. A different society developed in the area that is today the states of Pennsylvania, Delaware, New Jersey, and New York.
7. These settlers became farmers of the fertile soil of the region.
8. The southern colonies included Virginia, Maryland, North Carolina, South Carolina, and Georgia.
9. The climate allowed them to grow tobacco and rice.
10. Merchants in England, Germany, and Spain purchased these crops.

(Answers are on page 247.)

Surf's up...

To learn more about *common nouns* and *proper nouns*, check out this site:

http://www.lovetolearnplace.com/Grammar/commonnouns.html

CONCRETE AND ABSTRACT NOUNS

Another way to group nouns is by whether they are ***concrete nouns*** or ***abstract nouns***. A ***concrete noun*** names something that can be touched or seen. Another name for a concrete noun is a ***countable noun***. We call this type of noun *countable* because it names something that can be counted. For example, the words *cat* and *pencil* are countable nouns because you can **count** cats and pencils.

two *cats*
five *pencils*

A concrete noun can be either a proper noun or a common noun. For instance, the common noun *teacher* and the proper noun *Ms. Garcia* are concrete nouns.

Let's look at a special type of concrete noun.

Collective Nouns

A concrete noun is used to describe a group of people or things that is considered a single unit, and is called a ***group noun*** or a ***collective noun***. Some examples are

family	group
glass	nation
jury	majority
team	band

By contrast, an ***abstract noun*** names an idea, a thought, or a feeling. In other words, it names something that cannot be touched or seen. Abstract nouns are sometimes called ***noncountable nouns*** because they name something that cannot be counted. For instance, you can't count *happiness*. ***Abstract*** or ***noncountable*** nouns are always common nouns.

Concrete Noun	**Abstract Noun**
Carlos	friendship
computer	humor
San Francisco	fear
butterfly	happiness

Later in this chapter, you will learn how nouns are used in sentences. It's important to understand and be able to identify concrete and abstract nouns so that you can properly use them. Abstract nouns are tricky because many people don't think of words such as *fear* and *humor* as nouns.

Surf's up...

Surf into this site for more information about *concrete nouns* and *abstract nouns*:

http://www.chompchomp.com/terms/abstractnoun.htm

We've learned to distinguish between ***abstract nouns*** and ***concrete nouns*** to identify ***group nouns*** or ***collective nouns***. The following exercise provides an opportunity to practice grouping nouns in this way.

BRAIN TICKLERS!
Set #3
CITIZENSHIP

Identify the noun or nouns in each sentence. Next determine whether they are abstract or concrete nouns. Single underline the ***abstract nouns*** and double underline the ***concrete nouns***. Then, decide whether each of the concrete nouns is a ***collective noun***. Write a "**C**" above each collective noun.

EXAMPLE:

Ms. Vu is our social studies teacher.

C
Our class is learning about citizenship.

1. Honesty and responsibility are traits of a good citizen.
2. Honesty means to treat people of all cultures fairly.
3. Your culture greatly determines how you live.
4. It can include language, customs, and religion.
5. An ethnic group is a group of people who share the same customs.
6. Responsibility is addressing problems that occur in our society.
7. Attending school and following school rules are also part of civic responsibility.
8. The United States is a *democracy*.
9. Citizens in a democracy vote to elect their representatives.
10. Education helps citizens to be better voters because they can read about and understand the problems facing their society.

(Answers are on page 248.)

You've looked at different ways to group nouns and, therefore, understand and identify them. Now let's see how the English language forms nouns to name either one or more than one person, place, thing, idea, animal, quality, or action.

SINGULAR AND PLURAL NOUNS

With the exception of abstract nouns, nouns can be singular or plural. A singular ***noun*** refers to a single person, place, thing, idea, animal, quality, or action. On the other hand, a ***plural noun*** refers to more than one person, place, thing, idea, animal, or action. Usually, you can make a noun *plural* just by adding an ***-s*** to the end of the word.

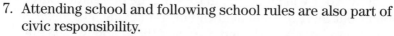

Singular	**Plural**
dog	dogs
book	books
camera	cameras

Unfortunately, not all English language nouns form their plurals so easily, and so you must learn a few rules to help you with those more difficult nouns.

Rule No. 1

If the last sound in the word is ***-s***, ***-ch***, ***-sh***, or ***-x***, you must add an ***-es*** to change the singular noun to a plural noun, and so that it can be easily pronounced. Below are some examples of these nouns and their plurals.

Singular	Plural
clas*s*	classes
mat*ch*	matches
di*sh*	dishes

Rule No. 1 will guide you in forming the plural for many nouns, but there are still many nouns remaining. For instance, many nouns end with the letter ***-y***, and these nouns have their own rule.

Rule No. 2

When a noun ends in a *consonant* followed by a ***-y***, to form the plural, you must drop the ***-y*** and add **-ies**. For example:

Singular	Plural
bab*y*	babies
lad*y*	ladies
countr*y*	countries

Rule No. 3

By contrast, if the final ***-y*** is preceded by a *vowel*, you form the plural by simply adding an ***-s***. Below are examples of nouns that follow this rule.

Singular	Plural
bo*y*	boys
donke*y*	donkeys
ba*y*	bays

You've learned how to form plurals when the noun ends in ***-s***, ***-ch***, ***-sh***, ***-x***, and ***-y***. Let's stop here and see how well you understand these rules for forming ***plural nouns***.

BRAIN TICKLERS!
Set #4
FREQUENTLY USED NOUNS

Use the rules presented in this section and a dictionary to help you change this list of frequently used nouns from ***singular nouns*** to ***plural nouns***. Write the plural of the singular noun on the line after it.

EXAMPLE:

toy *toys*

watch *watches*

1. church	____________	6. word	____________
2. flower	____________	7. house	____________
3. wish	____________	8. speech	____________
4. birthday	____________	9. family	____________
5. day	____________	10. school	____________

(Answers are on page 248.)

Let's look at some nouns whose plurals are a bit more difficult to form. Don't worry, though, there is a rule to help you.

Rule No. 4

For most nouns ending in ***-fe*** or ***-f,*** you can form the plural by first dropping the ***-fe*** or ***-f*** and then adding a ***-v*** and an ***-es***. Below are some examples.

Singular	**Plural**
wife	wi<u>ves</u>
scarf	scar<u>ves</u>
leaf	lea<u>ves</u>

This rule covers most of the nouns ending in ***-fe*** or ***-f***. Nevertheless, there are a few nouns ending in ***-f*** that form their plurals just by adding an ***-s***. For instance, *chief* becomes *chiefs*.

Some of the other nouns ending in ***-f*** that form their plurals by adding an ***-s*** are: **belief**, **reef**, **cliff**, **cuff**, **proof**, **roof**, **scruff**, **staff**, **surf**, and **whiff**.

Nouns ending with an ***-o*** are a little confusing when it comes to writing their plurals. Unfortunately, you don't have a rule to help you with these words. You will have to check the dictionary to learn the plural form. Some end in ***-s,*** while others end in ***-es***.

Singular	**Plural**
tomato	tomatoes
piano	pianos

Some nouns, whether they are written in the singular or the plural, have the same spelling. The nouns below are examples of these nouns.

Singular	**Plural**
deer	deer
fish	fish

Finally, some nouns completely change their spelling rather than merely add an ***-s*** or ***-es*** to form their plurals. As with the previous group of nouns, you'll need your dictionary to help you. Below are some examples of these nouns.

Singular	**Plural**
man	men
foot	feet
child	children

Surf's up...

The following web site provides examples for forming *plural nouns*:

http://www.quia.com/mc/67715.html

Some Unusual Nouns

You've learned some rules to help you write the plural of a noun, but you're not quite through. The English language has some unusual nouns when it comes to singular nouns and plural nouns. The following nouns don't have a plural:

furniture	sugar	air
hardware	flour	water
money	dust	timber

On the other hand, the nouns listed below are <u>always</u> plural:

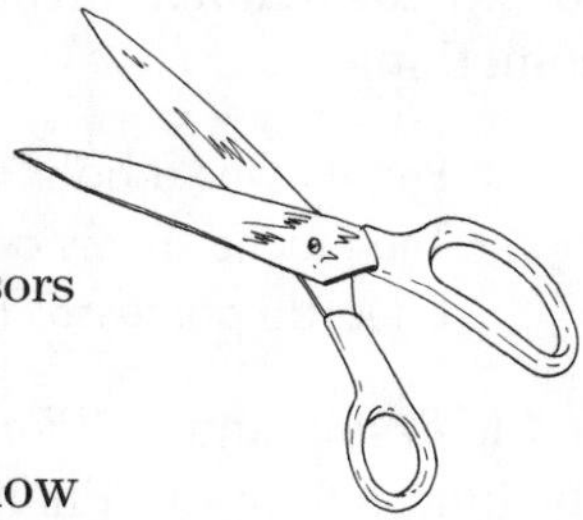

trousers	cattle	scissors
clothes	fruit	

The last few pages have shown you how some nouns form their plurals. The following exercise will give you a chance to review creating **noun plurals**.

BRAIN TICKLERS!
Set #5
MORE FREQUENTLY USED NOUNS

Use the rules mentioned in this section and a dictionary to help you change this list of frequently used nouns from ***singular nouns*** to ***plural nouns***. Write the plural of the singular noun on the line after it.

EXAMPLE:

window <u>windows</u>
life <u>lives</u>

1. tomato	________	6. leaf	________
2. knife	________	7. thief	________
3. half	________	8. man	________
4. mouse	________	9. radio	________
5. rodeo	________	10. self	________

(Answers are on page 248.)

You've learned about ***singular nouns*** and ***plural nouns***. Now, it's time to learn how nouns show they *own* or *possess* something.

POSSESSIVE NOUNS

Possessive nouns are important because you need to be able to express that a noun *owns* something, that is, it *possesses* something.

Pham owns a boat = *Pham's* boat
The teacher owns a house = the *teacher's* house
Eduardo possesses courage = *Eduardo's* courage

In the first example, *Pham's* is a possessive noun. It shows that the boat belongs to Pham. Similarly, in the second example, *teacher*'s is a possessive noun. It tells you that the *teacher* owns a *house*. Finally, the third example shows how you can write that *Eduardo* possesses a *quality*. That quality is *courage*.

As you've seen, a *possessive noun* shows ownership, that is, something belongs to that noun. To make a singular noun possessive, add an *apostrophe* and then add an ***-s***. For example:

Singular Noun	**Possessive Noun**
girl	girl's
Ugo	Ugo's
teacher	teacher's

To make a plural noun possessive, check the last letter—if the noun ends in ***-s***, add an *apostrophe* after it to show possession. If it doesn't, add an *apostrophe* and then add an ***-s***. The examples below illustrate this.

Plural Noun	**Possessive Plural Noun**
dogs	dogs'
children	children's
wives	wives'
Jones	Jones'

The following exercise will help you make sure you understand ***possessive nouns***.

BRAIN TICKLERS!

Set #6

FREQUENTLY USED POSSESSIVE NOUNS

Write the ***possessive form*** of each of the nouns below. Write your answer on the line on the right.

EXAMPLE:

deer <u>deer's</u>

cafeteria <u>cafeteria's</u>

cafeterias <u>cafeterias'</u>

1. tigers ____________
2. tree ____________
3. Ms. Jones ____________
4. thief ____________
5. thieves ____________
6. leaf ____________
7. leaves ____________
8. teachers ____________
9. baker ____________
10. Maria ____________

(Answers are on page 249.)

Surf's up...

Glide into this site for more information on *possessive nouns*:

http://grammar.uoregon.edu/case/possnouns.html

Using Multiple Possessive Nouns

Now that you understand how to write a ***possessive noun***, let's look at how you speak and write when you have more than one noun possessing something.

Possessive Noun Series

First, notice the situation that is called a ***possessive noun series***. A ***possessive noun series*** is the term used when you have more than one noun possessing the **same thing**. In this situation, you show each noun possessing the thing simply by writing the last noun in the series as a possessive. In other words, a single possessor requires only a single possessive.

> Incorrect
> Ms. Nguyen is *Juanita's* and *Sara's* teacher.

This sentence is incorrectly written because both *Juanita* and *Sara* possess *Ms. Nguyen* as their teacher. Since this is the case, only the *last* noun in the sentence needs to show possession.

> Correct
> Ms. Nguyen is *Juanita* and *Sara's* teacher.

This sentence is correctly written because the noun being possessed (*Ms. Nguyen*) only requires the single possessive (*Sara's*).

> *Incorrect*
> *Rachel's* and *Shirley's* trip was fun.

This sentence is incorrectly written because *Rachel* and *Shirley* had fun on the same *trip*. Instead of writing the sentence with two possessive nouns, you should show possession only with the last noun *(Shirley)*. The possessive noun *(trip)* requires only a single possessive (*Shirley's*).

> Correct
> *Rachel* and *Shirley's* trip was fun.

How do you know that *Rachel* and *Shirley* went on the same *trip*? The answer is in how the sentence is written. Had they gone on separate field trips, the sentence would have read:

> Rachel's and Shirley's *trips were* fun.

The noun *trip* would have been written in the plural.

Multiple Nouns Possessing Something Different

The other situation that you have with multiple possessive nouns is where each of the nouns possesses something different. In this case, each noun must show possession.

Incorrect
Juan and *Charlie's* shoes are very dirty.

This sentence is incorrectly written because both *Juan* and *Charlie* own dirty shoes. Consequently, both *Juan* and *Charlie* each must show possession.

Correct
Juan's and *Charlie's* shoes are very dirty.

Incorrect
The *Jones* and the *Smiths'* houses are in San Francisco.

This sentence is incorrectly written because both the *Jones* and the *Smiths* each own a house in San Francisco; therefore, both nouns must show possession.

Correct
The *Jones'* and the *Smiths'* houses are in San Francisco.

Again, to review, how would the sentence have been written if both the *Jones* and the *Smiths* owned the same house? The answer is the noun *house* would have been written in the singular.

The Jones and the Smiths' *house* is in San Francisco.

You have learned quite a lot about ***possessive nouns***. Before you continue, let's make sure you understand them.

BRAIN TICKLERS!
Set #7
USING POSSESSIVE NOUNS

Each of the sentences below contains ***possessive nouns.*** If the sentence is correct as it is written, write a "**C**" on the line provided. If the sentence is incorrect as it is written, write an **"I"** on the line provided and then rewrite the sentence so that it is correct.

EXAMPLE:

Mama Lisa is Pablo and Maria's grandmother. **C**

Hong and Van's cars are parked in their driveways. **I**

Hong's and *Van's* cars are parked in their driveways.

1. Mr. Parsons is Alfredo and Jesse's soccer coach. ____________
2. Let's go over to John's and Sally's house. ____________
3. Bill and Obi's pants are blue. ____________
4. The Tigers and the Lions' uniforms look similar. ____________
5. Ms. Jones, Mr. Clark's, and Ms. Kelly's classes were cancelled. ____________
6. Sandy's and Kelly's fathers are police officers. ____________

7. Ricky is Henry and Bobby's brother. ____________________

____

8. Roberta is Selena Pena's and Juan Pena's daughter. ________

____

9. Rex is Tito and Frank's dog. ____________________

____

10. Roman's and Jill's bus rides were exciting. ____________

____

(Answers are on page 249.)

FUNCTIONS OF NOUNS IN SENTENCES

You have learned what nouns are and how to form their plurals. In addition, you have studied how to change nouns so that they show possession. These skills will help you understand English and be understood when you speak and write in English. Another skill you should learn is: *How to use nouns.*

Nouns are used many ways in the English language. To discuss these ways, you have to know a bit about **verbs**, another one of the eight parts of speech listed at the beginning of this chapter. You will learn all about them in Chapter Three. Nevertheless, for right now, let's just say that verbs are words that show *action.* If you're still not too sure about verbs, you might want to jump ahead and skim Chapter Three on verbs and then come back here.

You can use nouns many ways in sentences. Let's look at four of the most common ways they are used.

1. As subjects of sentences

First, nouns can be the ***subjects*** of sentences. A *sentence* is a group of words that tells a complete thought. The subject is the noun or pronoun (See Chapter Two) and all the words that describe whom or what the sentence is about.

The *lion* ran through the tall grass.

The noun *lion* is the subject of the sentence because the rest of the sentence is telling you about the *lion*. Now you know the lion ran through the tall grass.

Our *teacher* is very nice.

The noun *teacher* is the subject of the sentence because the *teacher* is about whom the rest of the sentence is telling you something. She *is very nice*.

Juan and *Vicente* love to play soccer.

The nouns *Juan* and *Vicente* are the subjects of the sentence because the rest of the sentence tells you about them. They love to play soccer.

2. As direct objects of sentences

Nouns can be ***direct objects*** of sentences. The direct object follows the verb and completes its meaning. A direct object answers the question *who* or *what*?

Alberto's father caught a *fish*.

The noun *fish* is the direct object. It answers the question: What did the subject of the sentence (*Alberto's father*) catch?

Pablo is my *brother*.

The noun *brother* is the direct object. It answers the question: *Who is Pablo?*

3. As indirect objects of sentences

Nouns can be ***indirect objects*** of sentences. An indirect object is the person for whom or to whom something is done or given. You will usually write it between the verb and the direct object.

Ms. Sanchez handed *José* the chalk.

The noun *José* is an indirect object because it tells you *to whom* Ms. Sanchez handed the chalk. In this sentence, it appears after the verb *handed* and before the direct object *chalk*.

> The students paid the *cashier* the money.

The noun *cashier* is an indirect object because it tells you *to whom* the students paid the money. Can you identify the verb and the direct object in the above sentence?

4. As objects of prepositions in sentences

Finally, nouns can be ***objects of prepositions*** in sentences. A *preposition* is a word that shows a *relationship* between a noun or pronoun and another noun or pronoun.

> The food is ***on*** *the table*.

In this sentence, *on* is a preposition. It shows the *relationship* between the two nouns, *food* and *table*. We refer to the noun or pronoun connected to the prepositional phrase as the object of the preposition. Here, *on the table* is a prepositional phrase, and the noun *table* is the object of the preposition, *on*.

If you want to learn a bit more about prepositions and prepositional phrases, you can skim over Chapter Five. You'll see in Chapter Five that every prepositional phrase begins with a preposition and ends with a noun or pronoun.

IMPORTANT!

A *phrase* is any group of related words that, unlike a sentence, has no subject-predicate combination. The words in a phrase act together so that the phrase itself functions as a single part of speech. A phrase can't stand alone as a sentence.

Prepositional phrases act as either adjectives or adverbs, which means they modify or tell about a noun in the sentence or a verb. Check out Chapter Four if you are unfamiliar with adjectives and adverbs.

The man in the black *pants* is my father.

The prepositional phrase *in the black pants* is acting as an adjective because it tells you something about the subject of the sentence, *the man*.

The students in the *class* cheered for their *teacher*.

This sentence contains two prepositional phrases. The first prepositional phrase *in the class* contains the noun *class*. The phrase acts as an adjective because it describes the subject of the sentence, *the students*. The second prepositional phrase *for their teacher* contains the noun *teacher*. This prepositional phrase acts as an adverb because it tells you the teacher is being *cheered*.

Surf's up...

While you surf through cyberspace, you can learn more about how *nouns* are used at this site:

http://www.io.com/~hcexres/tcm1603/acchtml/twsent.html

You have learned four of the ways ***nouns*** are used in the English language. The exercise below will give you an opportunity to make sure you understand these important functions that nouns perform.

BRAIN TICKLERS!
Set #8
HURRICANES

Underline all of the ***nouns*** in the sentences below. Notice that one of the nouns is already double underlined. Write the type of ***noun*** (**subject**, **direct object**, **indirect object**, or an **object of the preposition**) on the line provided at the end of the sentence that has been double underlined.

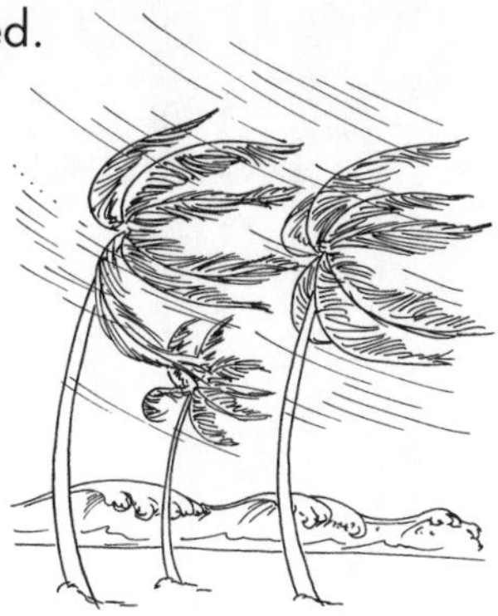

EXAMPLE:

Hurricanes are severe tropical storms. **subject**

In the fall, hurricanes strike the southeastern United States. **direct object**

1. The storms form in the southern Atlantic Ocean, the Caribbean Sea, and the Gulf of Mexico. ___________
2. In the northern hemisphere, hurricanes rotate in a counterclockwise direction around an "eye." ___________
3. When they come onto land, the heavy rain, strong winds, and heavy waves can damage buildings, homes, and cars. ___________
4. The heavy waves are called a *storm surge.* ___________
5. Storm surges are very dangerous and are the main reason why you must stay away from the ocean during a hurricane. ___________
6. A *meteorologist* studies the weather. ___________
7. Meteorologists have been studying hurricanes for about one hundred years. ___________
8. Evidence indicates that hurricanes have been occurring for several centuries. ___________

9. The Mayan word "Hurakan" became our word "hurricane."

____

10. Their god *Hurakan* blew his breath across the water.

____

(Answers are on page 249.)

This completes our discussion of one of the most important parts of speech, the noun. The next chapter will talk about a part of speech that is closely related to the noun—the ***pronoun***.

CHAPTER TWO

Pronouns

Pronouns are the simple, everyday words used in place of the names of people, places, or things. By using a pronoun, you can refer to people, places, or things that have already been mentioned by the speaker or writer without using the same noun every time.

For example, you would say:

> Without Pronouns:
> Tricia thinks that Johnny should lend Johnny's textbook to Johnny's cousin.
>
> With Pronouns:
> Tricia thinks that *he* should lend *his* textbook to *his* cousin.

There are only fifty pronouns in the English language, but that doesn't mean they aren't important. In fact, of the twenty-five most commonly used words in the English language, ten of them are pronouns! Pronouns are important, and because they are used so frequently, many times they are misused. The purpose of this chapter is to learn about pronouns and how to use them correctly.

WHAT IS A PRONOUN?

A ***pronoun*** is a word that takes the place of a noun. As with nouns, pronouns perform a variety of jobs in the English language, and just as you did with nouns, you can group pronouns based on those jobs they perform. Let's begin by looking at one of the most used group of pronouns, the ***personal pronouns***.

PERSONAL PRONOUNS

Personal pronouns can take the place of proper and common nouns that represent one or more persons or things. Examples of some personal pronouns are:

I	me
she	he
it	we

us
you

they
them

Personal pronouns make writing and speaking in English easier. For instance, if your name is *Maria*, you could write:

> *Maria* went to school this morning.

However, you usually don't refer to yourself by your name. Rather, you would simply write:

> *I* went to school this morning.

In this sentence, the personal pronoun *I* takes the place of the proper noun *Maria*.

Similarly, if you were writing about *Juan*, you might write:

> *Juan* wanted to go to the zoo, but the zoo was closed.

You could also write:

> *He* wanted to go to the zoo, but the zoo was closed.

In the above sentence, the personal pronoun *he* takes the place of *Juan*.

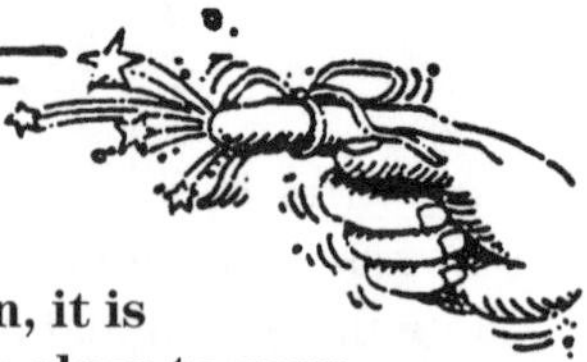

IMPORTANT!

Before you substitute a pronoun for a noun, it is important to think about whether it will be clear to your reader about *whom* or *what* you are writing. If you think the pronoun might confuse your reader, use the noun.

Suppose Maria wanted to tell you what Juan and she wanted to do. She could write:

> *Maria* and *Juan* wanted to go to the movies on Saturday.

Alternatively, by using personal pronouns, she could write:

> *He* and *I* wanted to go to the movies on Saturday.

In this sentence the personal pronouns *he* and *I* take the place of the proper nouns *Juan* and *Maria*.

You can also use personal pronouns to talk or write about *things*.

> Ugo wanted to go to the zoo, but the zoo was closed.

This sentence can also be written:

> Ugo wanted to go to the zoo, but *it* was closed.

In this rewritten sentence, the personal pronoun *it* took the place of *the zoo*.

Pronouns can also replace a noun and a pronoun that are connected in a sentence.

> *Ugo and I* are working on social studies homework.

This sentence becomes:

> *We* are working on social studies homework.

The personal pronoun *we* replaces the proper noun *Ugo* and the pronoun *I*.

Similarly, you could have the following sentence.

> Ms. Garcia gave *Carlos* and *him* some chocolate chip cookies.

Using a pronoun, you could write:

> Ms. Garcia gave *them* some chocolate chip cookies.

Here, the personal pronoun *them* replaces the proper noun *Carlos* and the pronoun *him*.

Work through the following exercise to make sure that you know how to use ***personal pronouns***.

BRAIN TICKLERS!
Set #1
LEARNING ABOUT CLIMATE

Notice the underlined noun or connected nouns and pronouns in each of the sentences below. Replace the underlined words in each sentence with a ***personal pronoun***.

EXAMPLE:

Ms. Vu teaches our class about geography.

She teaches our class about geography.

Carlos and Luis are working on a geography project assigned by Ms. Vu.

They are working on a geography project assigned by Ms. Vu.

1. I enjoy Ms. Vu's class. ______________________

   ____

2. Sometimes Ms. Vu allows each of us to pick something we would like to learn about. ______________________

   ____

3. Carlos and Luis are learning about the climate of the southeastern United States. ______________________

   ____

4. Ms. Vu told our class that *climate* is the weather conditions that occur throughout a particular region over a period, like a year. ______________________

   ____

5. Carlos is not sure which states are in the southeastern United States. ______________________

   ____

6. Luis and I looked in our geography book to find the answer.

   ____

7. Before we could find the answer, Rebecca and Sara told us the states in the southeastern United States include Alabama, Georgia, Florida, North Carolina, South Carolina, and Tennessee. ______________________

8. Ms. Vu told Carlos and me that some areas of the southeastern United States are experiencing a drought.

   ____

9. "A drought is a lack of moisture over a sizable area because it has rained very little," Ms. Vu explained.

   ____

10. A drought hurts the people, animals, and plants because people, plants, and animals need water to live and grow.

    ____

(Answers are on page 250.)

Surf's up...

Glide on into this site to learn more about *personal pronouns*:

http://grammar.uoregon.edu/pronouns/personal.html

Now that you understand the basics of personal pronouns, you need to learn how to use them properly. Namely, you need to know which pronouns to use as *subjects* of sentences and which pronouns to use as *objects* of sentences. That means you need to learn about ***pronoun cases.***

PRONOUN CASES

To speak and write English correctly, you select different pronouns depending on their ***case***, that is, how they are to be used in a phrase, clause, or sentence. In the English language, there are three main cases: the *subjective* case, the *objective* case, and the *possessive* case. When pronouns are acting as *subjects* of sentences, you must use ***subjective*** case pronouns. By contrast, when pronouns are acting as *direct objects*, *indirect objects*, or *objects of prepositions*, use pronouns in the ***objective*** case. Finally, whenever you want to show *ownership* of something, you must use pronouns in the ***possessive*** case. Many people misuse pronouns because they get confused as to which case the sentence is written. It's really quite simple to figure out, however. Let's begin by looking at the subjective and objective cases.

Subjective and Objective Cases

With nouns, the subjective and objective cases aren't a problem because nouns have the same form whether they are subjects or objects. In the example below, notice how the noun *girl* does not change regardless of whether it's a *subject* or a *direct object.*

> The *girl* hit the ball.

The noun *girl* is the <u>subject</u> of the sentence.

> The ball hit the *girl*.

In this sentence, the noun *girl* is a <u>direct object</u>.

Some pronouns, however, take different forms depending on whether they are *subjects* or *objects*. The following chart will help you to see the differences. Refer to it when you read the following examples and when you work the exercise at the end of this section.

Number	Person	Subjective Case	Objective Case
Singular	First	I	me
	Second	you	you
	Third	he, she, it	him, her, it
Plural	First	we	us
	Second	you	you
	Third	they	them
Relative pronoun		who, whoever	whom, whomever

Pronouns in the Subjective Case

For example, when you talk about yourself as a subject, you must use the pronoun *I*. However, if you are acting as an object in the sentence, you must use the pronoun *me*.

Incorrect
Me went to the store with my mother.

Writing this sentence using the pronoun *me* is incorrect because the pronoun in this sentence is the subject of the sentence, and so you need to use a pronoun in the *subjective case*, not one in the *objective case*.

Correct
I went to the store with my mother.

This sentence is written correctly because the pronoun *I* is the subject of the sentence, and *I* is a *subjective case* pronoun.

When you write a sentence that has **compound subjects**, that is, more than one subject, don't be confused. Pronouns should still be in the *subjective case*.

My brother and *I* went to the store.

The sentence has two subjects the noun *brother* and the pronoun *I*. The pronoun must be written in the *subjective case*.

IMPORTANT!

To keep from making pronoun case errors in sentences with compound subjects, drop the subject that is a noun and read the sentence with the pronoun alone. For instance, take the sentence:

My *mother* and *me* went to the store.

Is this sentence written correctly? To find out, read the sentence with the pronoun *me* alone.

***Me* went to the store.**

That doesn't sound right, and it's not correct English. It should be written:

***I* went to the store.**

Therefore, our original sentence should be written:

My mother and *I* went to the store.

Pronouns Following the Verb *To Be*

Examples of verbs that are a form of *to be* are: ***am***, ***are***, ***is***, ***was***, ***were*** and ***will be***. The pronoun after a form of the verb *to be* is called a **complement**. Complements must be written in the *subjective case.*

It is *I* who lost the book.

The verb *is* is a form of the *to be* verb. Consequently, the complement (pronoun) must be in the subjective case, which means that you need to use the pronoun *I*, rather than the objective case pronoun *me*.

The girl who correctly answered all of the questions was *she*.

The verb *was* is a form of the *to be* verb. To correctly write this sentence, use the subjective case pronoun *she*, rather than the objective case pronoun *her*.

Unlike words following action verbs, a complement of a linking verb is not an object, a receiver of action. Instead, the complement *identifies* or *refers to* the subject. Compare the following two sentences.

The teacher called Ms. Sanchez.

Ms. Sanchez is an object that receives the teacher's action of *calling*. If a pronoun were to be substituted for *Ms. Sanchez*, the pronoun would have to be written in the objective case: *her*.

The teacher called *her*.

Now look at:

The teacher is Ms. Sanchez.

Ms. Sanchez isn't receiving any action. Rather, the *to be* verb *is* identifies *Ms. Sanchez* as *the teacher*. Consequently, the correct pronoun for *Ms. Sanchez* in this sentence is *she*.

The teacher is *she*.

Surf's up...

Take a break and glide into this site on *pronoun cases*:

http://owl.english.purdue.edu/handouts/grammar/g_proncase.html

Pronouns in the Objective Case

Incorrect
Sara made cookies for Jane and *she*.

In this sentence, *Sara* is the subject. *Jane* and *she* are objects of the preposition *for*. However the sentence is incorrectly written because the pronoun *she* is a pronoun in the *subjective case*. You need to use a pronoun that is in the *objective case*.

Correct
Sara made cookies for Jane and her.

This sentence is correctly written because the pronoun *her* is in the *objective case.*

Selecting the correct pronoun case can sometimes be a bit tricky. Use the following exercise to make sure you understand ***pronoun cases***.

BRAIN TICKLERS!
Set #2
LEARNING ABOUT BUTTERFLIES

Read each of the following sentences. If the underlined pronoun or pronouns are written in the correct ***case***, write a **C** on the line following the sentence. If the pronouns are written in the incorrect case, write an **I** on the line following the sentence, and then rewrite the sentence so that the pronouns are in the proper case.

EXAMPLE:

Sara and her are in my science class. **I** ______

Sara and *she* are in my science class.

1. John and me are learning about butterflies in science class.

   ______

2. Ms. Garcia told we that butterflies have three body parts: a head, a thorax, and an abdomen. ______

   ______

3. I asked her what a "thorax" was. ______

   ______

4. Her said it was the butterfly's chest. ____________________

____

5. "Whom knows where the abdomen is?" asked Ms. Garcia.

____

6. "It is the tail part," I said. ____________________

____

7. Van and me counted the number of legs on the butterfly.

____

8. Us counted six legs. ____________________

____

9. "Butterflies have two sets of two wings," Van said to I. ____

____

10. We noticed the wings and legs were connected to the thorax.

____

(Answers are on page 250.)

Now that you are familiar with *subjective* and *objective* pronouns, let's learn about the remaining case of pronouns—***possessive pronouns.***

POSSESSIVE PRONOUNS

You can use ***possessive pronouns*** to show *ownership* of something. You learned in Chapter One that adding an apostrophe forms the possessive case of nouns.

Bob's desk is messy.
The *cat's* claws are sharp.
Our *dogs'* bowls are filled with water and food.

By contrast, *possessive pronouns* completely change their spelling to show possession or ownership. The following table shows the personal pronouns in their cases. Notice there are two sets of possessive pronouns: one for writing before the noun in the sentence and the other for writing after the noun in the sentence.

CASE

Number	Person	Subjective	Objective	Possessive	
				Before the noun	After the noun
Singular	First	I	me	my	mine
	Second	you	you	your	yours
	Third	he	him	his	his
		she	her	her	hers
		it	it	its	it
Plural	First	we	us, ours	our	ours
	Second	you	you	your	yours
	Third	they	them	their	theirs
Relative pronoun		who	whom	whose	whose
Indefinite pronoun		everybody	everybody	everybody's	everybody's

I saw *her* mother in the store.

You need to use the possessive pronoun *her* because it appears <u>before</u> the noun it is possessing *mother*.

The mother in the store is *hers*.

By contrast, here you should use the possessive pronoun *hers* because it appears <u>after</u> the noun it is possessing in the sentence *mother*.

Is this *your* backpack?

In this sentence, use the possessive pronoun *your* because it appears <u>before</u> the noun it is possessing, *backpack*. Notice the following sentence.

Is this backpack *yours*?

Here, *yours* is the correct possessive pronoun to use in this sentence because it appears <u>after</u> the noun it possesses, *backpack*.

Its and It's

The following example will help you with a possessive pronoun that sometimes confuses people.

What is *its* name?

Here, use the possessive pronoun *its* to show possession of the noun *name*. Do not confuse the possessive pronoun *its* with *it's*, which is the contraction of it is. For example, here you would write:

It's time to eat lunch. (*It is* time to eat lunch.)

By contrast, you would write the following sentence:

The old coin had lost *its* shine.

Surf's up...

Here's a great web site about *possessive pronouns*:

http://englishplus.com/grammar/00000023.htm

Using ***possessive pronouns*** can be a bit tricky. Work through the following exercise to make sure you can use them correctly.

BRAIN TICKLERS!

Set #3

PETS

For each sentence, fill in the blank with the correct ***possessive pronoun***. Select the correct possessive pronoun from the pronouns in the parentheses following each sentence.

Once you have selected the correct possessive pronoun, write the entire sentence in the line under the sentence.

EXAMPLE:

"Is this dog ______?" Joes asked me. (your, yours)

"Is this dog *yours*?" Joe asked me.

"Yes, that is _____ dog," I answered. (my, mine)

"Yes, that is *my* dog," I answered.

1. A dog is ______ family's pet. (our, ours)

   ____

2. _______ name is Heidi. (Her, Hers)

   ____

3. ______ father told me that Heidi belongs to a *breed* or type of dog known as a German shepherd. (My, Mine)

   ____

4. _______ fur is black and brown in color. (Her, Hers)

   ____

5. Our neighbors, the Garzas, have a cat as ________ pet. (their, theirs)

   ____

6. _________ textbook has some interesting facts about cats. (Our, Ours)

   ____

7. ______ eyes see better in the dark than humans' eyes. (Their, Theirs)

   ____

8. However, our eyes see better than _______ in daylight. (their, theirs)

____

9. _______ cat's sense of smell is fourteen times stronger than your own. (Your, Yours)

____

10. _______ whiskers spread out roughly as wide as its body making it able to judge if it can fit through an opening. (It's, Its)

____

(Answers are on page 250.)

Now that you know about personal pronouns and their case, let's learn about another group of pronouns that are closely connected to personal pronouns—***reflexive pronouns***.

REFLEXIVE PRONOUNS

Reflexive pronouns are used to *reflect* or *refer back* to nouns or pronouns in the sentence. A reflexive pronoun is usually used when the *object* of a sentence is the same as the *subject* of the sentence. You write reflexive pronouns by combining some of the personal pronouns with the endings ***–self*** (singular pronouns) or ***–selves*** (plural pronouns).

Pronoun		Reflexive Pronoun
Subjective	**Objective**	
I	me	myself
you	you	yourself
he	him	himself
she	her	herself
it	it	itself
us	we	ourselves
they	them	themselves

He surprised *himself.*

In this sentence, the reflexive pronoun *himself* refers to the subject pronoun *he.*

When Carla was playing with the scissors, *she* accidentally cut *herself.*

Here, the reflexive pronoun *herself* refers to the subject pronoun *she.*

Reflexive pronouns are quite useful, but you need to be careful. They should never be used as *subjects* or *objects.*

Incorrect
Juan and *myself* like to listen to music.

This sentence is incorrectly written because the reflexive pronoun *myself* is used as one of the subjects of the sentence. Instead, use a subjective pronoun.

Correct
Juan and *I* like to listen to music.

The sentence is now correctly written because the subjective pronoun *I* is used as a subject along with the proper noun *Juan.*

Incorrect
The cat hissed at my sister and *myself.*

This sentence is incorrectly written because the reflexive pronoun *myself* is being used as a direct object. Instead, use an objective pronoun.

Correct
The cat hissed at my sister and *me.*

The sentence is now correct because you have used the objective pronoun *me.*

Although they can be tricky, ***reflexive pronouns*** come in handy when writing and speaking. Work through the following exercise to make sure you understand them.

BRAIN TICKLERS!
Set #4
A Trip to the Zoo

For each sentence, choose the correct pronoun in the parentheses following each sentence and write it in the blank provided. Use ***reflexive pronouns*** wherever possible.

EXAMPLE:

The four of _____ decided to visit the zoo. (us, ourselves)

The four of _us_ decided to visit the zoo.

I gave _______ a headache by trying to look at all the animals at once. (me, myself)

I gave _myself_ a headache by trying to look at all the animals at once.

1. The female tiger was in a cage by __________. (her, herself)
2. We __________ were not afraid of the tiger because she was in a cage. (us, ourselves)
3. The big cat growled at my friends and _______. (me, myself)
4. The elephants helped __________ to some food. (them, themselves)
5. The zoo worker _________ gave the elephants hay and vegetables to eat. (he, himself)
6. Because they are in a zoo, the elephants can't get food _________. (them, themselves)

7. I __________ would like to take care of the elephants. (me, myself)
8. "So would ______," said Rosa. (I, myself)

9. "________, I would rather feed the tigers," said Roman. (Me, Myself)
10. We agreed among _______ to come back to the zoo. (us, ourselves)

(Answers are on page 250.)

Now that you are familiar with reflexive pronouns, you can learn about another group of pronouns—***demonstrative pronouns***.

DEMONSTRATIVE PRONOUNS

The ***demonstrative pronouns*** (**this, that, these, those**) stand in for the name of a person, place, or thing that must be pointed to. In fact, you can call these **pointer pronouns**. Using them is like *pointing* to the person, place, or thing that you are talking or writing about. The demonstrative pronouns ***this*** and ***these*** refer to things that are *nearby* either in time or space. By comparison, the demonstrative pronouns ***that*** and ***those*** refer to things that are *distant* in time or space.

> *This* restaurant we're entering serves good food. (pointing to a restaurant)
> *That* was my brother you met last week. (pointing to a person)
> *These* shoes are nicer than the ones I saw in the store yesterday. (pointing to a pair of shoes)
> Show me *those* on the top shelf. (pointing to a something at a location)

> Incorrect
> *That* plate I'm holding is hot.

This sentence is incorrectly written because the demonstrative pronoun *that* should be used when referring to something distant.

> Correct
> *This* plate I'm holding is hot.

Here, the sentence is correctly written because the plate is nearby, and so you must use the demonstrative pronoun *this*.

Surf's up...

If you want to learn more about *demonstrative pronouns*, try this site:

http://www.uottawa.ca/academic/arts/writcent/hypergrammar/pronouns.html

Now it's time to work through the following exercise to practice using ***demonstrative pronouns***.

BRAIN TICKLERS!

Set #5

SPIDERS

In the sentences below, choose the correct ***demonstrative pronoun*** (**this**, **that**, **these**, **those**) to replace the underlined words in each sentence. Rewrite the sentence using the correct demonstrative pronoun.

EXAMPLE:

"The spiders in the terrarium over there look scary!" said my cousin. (That, Those)

"*Those* look scary!" said my cousin.

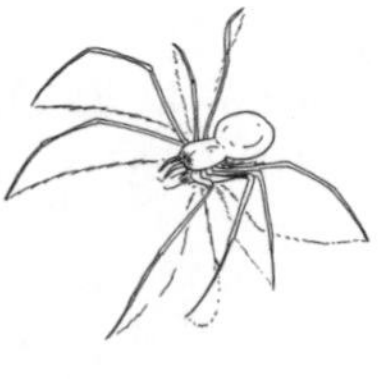

I just saw one crawl straight up the wall in the kitchen. (those, that)

I just saw one crawl straight up *that.*

1. <u>The lynx spiders in that terrarium in the corner</u> are just one of 40,000 kinds of spiders in the world. (That, Those)

 ____

2. As we looked at a poster on the wall displaying the spider's segmented legs, Pedro said, "All spiders have <u>segmented legs</u>." (that, those)

 ____

3. "<u>Thick brushes of hair</u> cover the end of each leg," Pedro explained, showing us a spider he had just taken from a terrarium. (These, This)

 ____

4. "<u>A tiny foot at the end of each leg</u> lets them walk up vertical surfaces, like walls," he continued as we looked at the spider's leg under the microscope. (This, That)

 ____

5. You can see only <u>their feet</u> when you look under a microscope. (this, these)

 ____

6. "Spiders feed mainly on <u>insects</u>," Pedro said as he held a jar of flies. (that, these)

 ____

7. "<u>Its web</u> enables it to catch insects," Pedro said, pointing to the spider on the far table spinning its web. (This, That)

 ____

8. Because they eat live things such as <u>insects in this jar</u>, spiders are *carnivores*. (that, these)

 ____

9. "What are <u>carnivores</u>?" I asked, pointing at the spider. (this, these)

 ____

10. "<u>Carnivores</u> are animals that eat other animals," answered Pedro. (This, These)

 ____

(Answers are on page 250.)

IMPORTANT!

The words *this, that, these,* and *those* can be confusing. When they replace nouns, these words are *demonstrative* pronouns. However, when they are written before nouns (*this* coat; *that* man; *these* people), *this, that, these,* and *those* are *adjectives*.

You have seen how demonstrative pronouns *described* the nouns they replaced. Now let's learn about a group of pronouns called ***relative pronouns***, which *introduce* nouns and personal pronouns.

RELATIVE PRONOUNS

The ***relative pronouns*** (**who**, **whom**, **which**, **that**) introduce clauses that describe nouns or pronouns.

> The student who wrote the story is reading it to the class.

The relative pronoun *who* introduces the clause *who wrote the story,* which describes the subject *student.* If you didn't have relative pronouns, you would have to write the sentence in this very awkward way to let your reader know what is going on.

> The student—the student wrote the story—is reading it to the class.

Here's another example:

> The building *that* stood on the corner has been torn down.

The clause *that stood on the corner* begins with the relative pronoun *that.* The clause tells you about the building. Again, without the relative pronoun *that,* you would have to write the sentence something like this:

> The building—the building on the corner—has been torn down.

The chart below shows you the types of nouns for which each of the relative pronouns can substitute.

Relative Pronoun	substitutes for	Nouns
who		persons
that		things, places (sometimes, people)
which		things, places

The teacher *who* was nice to me yesterday waved to me today.
The airplane *that* flew in from Mexico is sitting on the runway.
The math problems, *which* I just finished, are completely right.

Notice that both *that* and *which* can substitute for nouns that are things or places. The problem is that you can't just pick one or the other. You must use *that* when the clause that follows it is *restrictive*, that is, when the clause is *necessary* to tell something important about the subject. Conversely, you need to use the relative pronoun *which* when the clause that follows it is *nonrestrictive*, that is, when it provides information that isn't important in telling us something about the subject.

Incorrect
The train, *which* ran off the tracks, was going very fast.

This sentence is incorrect because *ran off the tracks* is important information describing this particular train. Because this clause provides important information, it is a *restrictive clause*. Restrictive clauses describing nouns that are things must be introduced by the relative pronoun *that*.

Correct
The train *that* ran off the tracks was going very fast.

Incorrect
The bridge *that* I travel over every day is closed.

The important fact about the bridge is that it is closed. Consequently, the fact that I travel over it every day is not that important; therefore, this particular clause referring to the bridge is a *nonrestrictive* clause. Consequently, the clause should begin with the relative pronoun *which*.

Correct

The bridge, *which I travel over every day*, is closed.

Now that you understand when to use *that* and when to use *which*, it's time to look at the other set of tricky relative pronouns, *who* and *whom.*

Earlier in this chapter, you read about pronouns being in the *subjective* or *objective* case. To review, a pronoun is in the *subjective* case whenever it is substituting for a noun that is the subject of the sentence. For example, in the following sentence, the pronoun *I* is in the subjective case because it is substituting for the person who is the subject of the sentence.

I am going to the school across from the post office.

A pronoun is in the *objective* case when it is substituting for a noun that is a direct object, an indirect object, or an object of a preposition. For example, in the sentence below, *me* is a direct object because *me* is receiving the direct action of the ball hitting.

The ball hit *me* on the nose.

When deciding whether to use *who* or *whom*, you must determine whether the noun to which the relative pronoun will be referring is in the *subjective case* or in the *objective case.* If the noun is in the *subjective case*, you should use the relative pronoun *who.*

The man *who* lives next door to me is my uncle.

Here, the relative pronoun *who* is referring to the subject of the sentence, *man.* By contrast, if the noun to which the relative pronoun will be referring is in the *objective case*, you should use the relative pronoun *whom.*

Ms. Garcia, to *whom* I handed my homework, just left.

The relative pronoun *whom* is substituting for the direct object of the sentence, *Ms. Garcia.*

Surf's up...

Do you need to review a bit more about *relative pronouns*? Check out this site:

http://grammar.uoregon.edu/pronouns/relative.html

Take a few minutes to work on the following exercise. It will give you an opportunity to use what you have learned about ***relative pronouns***.

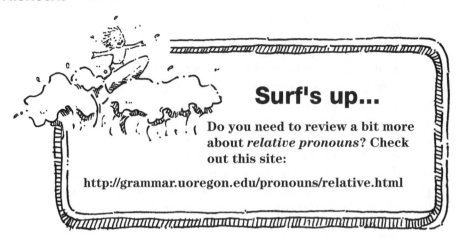

BRAIN TICKLERS!

Set #6

USING RELATIVE PRONOUNS

In the sentences below, choose the correct ***relative pronoun*** from the pronouns in the parentheses at the end of each of the sentences. Insert the correct relative pronoun in the blank.

EXAMPLE:

The road ______ is closed is the one I take home. (that, which)

The road *that* is closed is the one I take home.

The girl _____ smiled at me yesterday is here. (who, whom)

The girl *who* smiled at me yesterday is here.

1. The man ______ picked me up from school is my Uncle Tito. (who, whom)
2. The car, ______ is green, is out of gas. (which, that)

3. The cat ______ bit me was a brown tabby. (which, that)
4. The girl ______ waved to me is my friend. (who, whom)
5. The girl, to ______ I waved, is my friend. (who, whom)
6. The man _____ is wearing the funny hat is my father. (who, whom)
7. The window, ______ is in the back of the house, is broken. (which, whom)
8. Ms. Jenkins, _______ I known well, is moving away from the neighborhood. (who, whom)
9. The lady ______ fell down is fine now. (who, whom)
10. My cousins, ______ I don't see very often, are coming to see me. (who, whom)

(Answers are on page 251.)

Relative pronouns serve an important function in the English language. Now, let's look at pronouns being used in another important way—as ***interrogative pronouns***.

INTERROGATIVE PRONOUNS

The ***interrogative pronouns*** (**who, whom, whose, which, what**) are usually used as the *beginnings* of questions.

Which backpack do you like better?
Who wants more ice cream?
To *whom* does this coat belong?
What time does the movie begin?
Whose name is on the winning raffle ticket?

Although they usually begin questions, interrogative pronouns can also be used *within* a sentence to ask a question. For instance,

Ms. Jones, our social studies teacher, wondered *who* would score the highest grade on her test.
As Luis got out of the car, his mother asked him *what* time he wanted her to pick him up.
The teacher didn't know *whose* lunch she was holding.

We couldn't catch the rabbit because we couldn't figure out <u>*which* way it would run</u>.

IMPORTANT!

If you are in doubt about using *who* or *whom*, substitute the words *he/she* and *him/her* in the sentence and determine which one sounds better. If *he/she* is correct, use *who*; however, if *him/her* sounds better, use *whom*.

Taking the earlier example:

***Who* wants more ice cream?**

First, substitute *him*:

***Him* wants more ice cream. (Not correct.)**

Next, substitute *he*:

***He* wants more ice cream. (Correct—use *who*.)**

The exercise below will give you some practice using ***interrogative pronouns***.

BRAIN TICKLERS!
Set #7
USING INTERROGATIVE PRONOUNS

In each of the sentences below, write an ***interrogative pronoun*** (**who**, **whom**, **whose**, **which**, **what**) in the blank that helps complete the sentence. Choose the correct answer from the two choices in the parentheses after each sentence.

EXAMPLE:

Tracy asked the boys <u>*whose*</u> team won the game. (who, whose)

My brother is the runner <u>*who*</u> won the marathon. (who, which)

1. Sara wanted to ask ________ student's drawing the judges liked the best. (whom, which)
2. ________ did you invite to the dance? (Who, Whom)
3. _______ car is parked in front of the school? (Whose, Who)
4. As soon as they entered the restaurant, the waiter asked them _______ they want to eat. (which, what)
5. ______ are you, and why are you here? (Who, Whom)
6. _______ do you think we should do? (Whose, What)
7. ________ music store do you like better? (Who, Which)
8. We couldn't figure out _____ was going to happen next. (what, which)
9. With _____ is Janet supposed to work? (who, whom)
10. _________ was his excuse for being late to school? (Which, What)

(Answers are on page 251.)

Surf's up...

Check out this site to learn more about *interrogative pronouns*:

http://grammar.uoregon.edu/pronouns/interrogative.html

You've seen the important function in the English language that interrogative pronouns perform. Now, let's look at another group of important pronouns—***indefinite pronouns***.

INDEFINITE PRONOUNS

An ***indefinite pronoun*** is a pronoun that replaces a noun without specifying which noun it replaces. Listed below are some examples of indefinite pronouns:

everyone	nothing	each
anyone	anything	some
something	either	nobody
somebody	none	no one
all	both	either
more	most	neither
many	few	several
little	plenty	least
less	much	lots

Does *anyone* know the answer to the first problem?

The indefinite pronoun *anyone* does not refer to a particular person; rather, it refers to an unspecified person in the group.

That is *more* than I wanted.

The indefinite pronoun *more* does not describe a particular quantity; rather, it makes a comparison.

Each has her toys in the bedroom.

The indefinite pronoun *each* does not name a particular child; however, you do know that the children have their toys in the bedroom.

The exercise below will give you an opportunity to use what you have learned about ***indefinite pronouns***.

BRAIN TICKLERS!

Set #8

USING A MAP

In each of the sentences below, <u>underline</u> the ***indefinite pronoun*** or ***pronouns***.

EXAMPLE:

<u>No one</u> likes to be lost when they are traveling somewhere.

That is why <u>everyone</u> should know how to read a map.

1. From reading a map, much can be learned.
2. All have a *scale* to show the distances between places.
3. Many are found in the *legend* or *map key.*
4. By using the scale, anyone can determine the distance between two points.
5. *Map distance* is something a scale tells us.
6. Anyone can determine the relationship between the *map distance* and the *real distance.*
7. Both can be related by using a *ratio*, which is a relationship between any two quantities.
8. For instance, a map might write its ratio as “1 inch equals 100 miles” or 1:100—both mean the same thing.
9. “Does anyone not understand the difference between *real distance* and *map distance*?” our teacher asked.
10. Using a ruler and knowing the scale, someone can accurately measure the distance between places.

(Answers are on page 251.)

Now that you are familiar with ***indefinite pronouns***, you need to learn an important rule about how to use them.

MAKING PRONOUNS AGREE

An important rule for writing and speaking English is that a pronoun must agree with its **antecedent**, the word to which it refers. In other words, the antecedent is the word you would have to repeat in a sentence if you couldn't use a pronoun. ***Agreement*** requires using a plural pronoun with a plural antecedent and using a singular pronoun with a singular antecedent. To make this easier, remember these rules:

- Use *his* or *her* if the antecedent is singular.
  Maria had lost *her* purse.
- Use the pronoun *their* if the antecedent is plural.
  The *players* were wearing *their* uniforms.

Although you have the above rules to help you, you can still run into problems making pronouns and their antecedents agree. Choosing the correct pronoun can be tricky when your antecedent is an ***indefinite pronoun*** rather than a noun as in the previous examples. It's tricky because some indefinite pronouns are *singular*, some are *plural*, and some are *both*. To help make sure your pronouns agree with your indefinite pronoun in the sentence, use the following chart, which shows whether the indefinite pronouns are singular, plural, or both. Refer to this chart when you are reading the following examples and working on the exercise at the end of this section.

Singular	Plural	Singular or Plural
anybody	few	all
anyone	many	any
each	several	either
everybody	lots	more
everyone	both	most

nobody	neither
somebody	none
someone	some
less	plenty
much	
no one	

Incorrect
Several lost *his or her* papers when the wind blew.

This sentence is incorrectly written because the pronoun *his or her* is singular; however, the antecedent *several* is plural.

Correct
Several lost *their* papers when the wind blew.

This sentence is correctly written because the plural pronoun *their* agrees with its plural antecedent *several.*

Incorrect
Each knows what *they* need to do.

This sentence is incorrect because the antecedent indefinite pronoun *each* is singular, but the pronoun *they* is plural.

Correct
Each knows what *he or she* needs to do.

This sentence is correct because the singular pronoun *he or she* agrees with its singular indefinite pronoun *Each.*

The following exercise will help you practice choosing the correct pronoun to agree with its ***indefinite pronoun*** antecedent.

BRAIN TICKLERS!
Set #9
WRITING WITH INDEFINITE PRONOUNS

Determine whether each of the sentences containing ***indefinite pronouns*** is correctly written. If it is, write a **C** on the line following the sentence. If it's not correctly written, write an **I** on the line following the sentence, and then rewrite the sentence so that it is correct.

EXAMPLE:

Several of the boys spent his time watching television. **I**

Several of the boys spent *their* time watching television.

Each of the girls sat at *her* desk. **C**

1. Anybody can write well if they work hard.

2. Few are in his or her room.

3. Nobody is done with their project.

4. Most of the students were finished with their assignments.

5. A few of the teachers drove their cars.

6. None of the women brought their lunches.

7. Someone left their cake out in the rain.

8. No one should have to read a story if it embarrasses him or her.

____

9. Each should write in his or her journal.

____

10. More should write in their journal.

____

(Answers are on page 251.)

Congratulations! You are finished with pronouns. Remember, they can take the place of nouns, which you learned about in Chapter One. Now it is time to for some action! That is, it's time to study words that describe action—***verbs***.

CHAPTER THREE

Verbs

Action movies. Action games. Action. Action. Action. We like action. Why? *Action* makes things interesting. So far, you have learned how to name people, places, and things with nouns and pronouns. But now it's time to put those nouns and pronouns into action. Doing so will make your writing interesting, and to do that, you need to learn about ***verbs***.

WHAT IS A VERB?

You learned in the first two chapters that a sentence contains two main parts: a *subject* and a *predicate.* The *subject* tells you whom or what the sentence is about. On the other hand, the *predicate* describes what the subject does or is.

The dog ran through our front yard.

In the above sentence, the subject of the sentence *the dog* is single underlined; whereas the predicate is double underlined. The job of a ***verb*** is to describe the **action** or express a **state of being**. The verb is always in the predicate. In the example sentence, the verb is *ran.* Let's talk about one of the jobs a verb performs—describing the *action* of the subject. It shouldn't surprise you that verbs such as *ran* that perform this job are called ***action verbs***. Let's look at some action verbs.

ACTION VERBS

Ms. Vu *sang* a song.

The action verb *sang* describes the action performed by the subject of the sentence. Here, *Ms. Vu* performed her action with a song. She *sang* it.

The girls *walked* around the mall.

The action verb *walked* describes what the subject of the sentence *the girls* did at the mall.

Here's one more example:

Roman *kicked* the soccer ball.

The action verb *kicked* tells us what the subject of the sentence *Roman* did with the soccer ball.

Surf's up...

If you want to learn more about *action verbs*, glide into this web site:

http://esl.vcc.ca/eslvoc/ESLWEB/verbs1.htm

Action verbs help you speak and write in a more interesting and exciting way. The following exercise will provide practice identifying sentences with these important words.

BRAIN TICKLERS!
Set #1
ROBOTS

Select the ***action verb*** from the list that best completes each sentence below and write it in the blank.

power	attached	roll
use	comes	walk

EXAMPLE

A robot is a machine with a computer brain that **moves** its body.

A robot is different from other machines that move because its computer brain **controls** its movements.

1. Robots differ from computers because computers don't have bodies _______ to them.
2. Some robots ______ on legs made of metal or plastic.

3. Others ________ along on motorized wheels.
4. Some robots _____ motors to help them move.
5. Small batteries inside the robot _______ these motors.
6. Our word *robot* ______ from the Czech word *robota*.

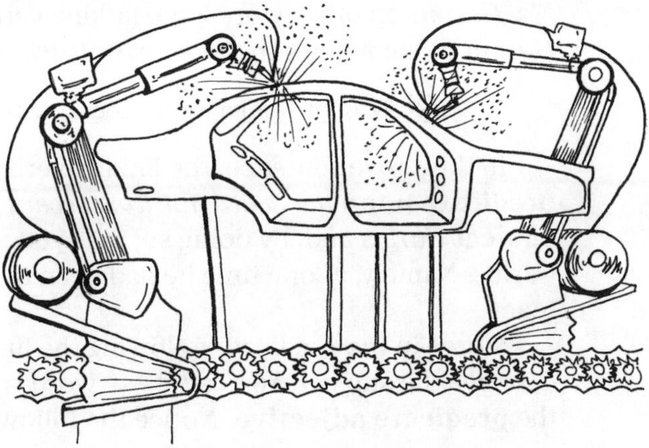

(Answers are on page 252.)

Although action verbs are important, there is another group of verbs that performs an important job. This group of verbs is called ***linking verbs***. Let's see what they do.

LINKING VERBS

Linking verbs *link* or *connect* the subject of the sentence to the predicate of the sentence. Rather than describing action, a linking verb helps the words following it to **refer** to the subject. Linking verbs describe no action—they merely state an existing condition or relationship. The most common linking verbs are some form of the verb "to be," such as **am**, **being**, **will be**, **can, be, have, is, are**, **was,** and **were**. Other common linking verbs are forms of **to seem, to appear**, **to feel**, **to taste**, **to look**, **to grow, to prove, to remain, to smell, to sound, to stay,** and **to become**.

How do linking verbs work? Sometimes, the words following the linking verb refer to the subject by *renaming* the subject. These words that follow the linking verb are known as a *predicate noun*. For instance,

Ms. Garcia *is* my social science teacher.

In the above sentence, the linking verb *is* helps the **predicate noun** *social science teacher* refer to the **subject**

Ms. Garcia. In other words, the linking verb **renames** *Ms. Garcia* as someone's *social science teacher.*

> Carlos *was* the goalie for his soccer team.

In the above sentence, the linking verb *was* helps the **predicate noun** *the goalie for his soccer team* rename the **subject** *Carlos* and, by doing so, tells you something more about Carlos. Namely, at one time he had been the goalie for his soccer team.

Words in the predicate following the linking verb can also *describe* the subject. You call these words describing the subject the **predicate adjective**. Notice the following sentence:

> The girls *are* happy.

The linking verb *are* helps the **predicate adjective** *happy* to describe the **subject** *girls.* The linking verb enables the writer to tell you about the girls. Namely, they are *happy.*

> Roman *feels* lonely.

Here the linking verb *feels* helps the **predicate adjective** *lonely* describe the **subject** *Roman.* Now you know something about the subject *Roman*—he is lonely.

IMPORTANT!

How do you tell if a verb is an action verb or a linking verb?

If you can substitute *am*, *is*, or *are* for the verb and the sentence still makes sense, you have a linking verb. On the other hand, if after the substitution, the sentence makes no sense, the verb is an action verb.

EXAMPLE

Take the sentence: Juan jumps over the fence.

Now substitute: Juan *is* over the fence. This sentence makes very little sense; therefore; *jumps* is an action verb.

Try the same test with: Samantha looks unhappy. Notice the difference?

The following exercise will give you practice identifying ***subjects***, ***predicates***, and ***linking verbs***, as well as ***predicate nouns*** and ***predicate adjectives***.

BRAIN TICKLERS!
Set #2
EARLY PRESIDENTS

For each of the following sentences, first identify the ***subject*** and the ***predicate.*** Single underline the ***subject*** and double underline the ***predicate.*** Next, write the ***linking verb*** on the first line following the sentence. On the second line following each sentence, write **PN** if the predicate is a ***predicate noun*** or **PA** if the predicate is a ***predicate adjective***.

EXAMPLE

George Washington became the first president of the United States.
became PN

He was courageous and honest. **was PA**

1. George Washington was born in Virginia. _____ _____
2. Our second president was John Adams. _____ _____
3. Thomas Jefferson, our third president, was the founder of the University of Virginia. _____ _____
4. Jefferson and Adams were lawyers. _____ _____
5. George Washington and Thomas Jefferson became famous. _____ _____
6. Both remain well respected. _____ _____

(Answers are on page 252.)

Surf's up...

Check out this site to learn more about *linking verbs*:

http://grammar.uoregon.edu/verbs/linking.htm

We all need some help from time to time, and so do verbs! Let's take a look at verbs that *help* other verbs. We call these verbs—simply enough—***helping verbs***.

HELPING VERBS

A ***helping verb*** is a verb that is added to another verb to make the meaning of the sentence clearer. Helping verbs include any form of the verb "to be" along with the following forms of common verbs: **can**, **could**, **do**, **does**, **have**, **has**, **had**, **may**, **might**, **must**, **shall**, **should**, **will**, **would, be, being, am, are, is, was, were,** and **did.**

Notice how adding a ***helping verb*** can change the meaning of a sentence.

Juan *may* study his vocabulary words tonight.
Juan *should* study his vocabulary words tonight.
Juan *can* study his vocabulary words tonight.
Juan *will* study his vocabulary words tonight.

Suppose Roman and you are going to play soccer. If you're sure that is what you are going to do, you will write

Roman and I *will* play soccer.

Notice how the helping verb *will* makes your playing soccer certain. However, if you are not sure you will be playing soccer, then you will write

Roman and I *might* play soccer.

Here, you are making it clear to the reader that it is <u>not certain</u> Roman and you will be playing soccer.

Surf's up...

If you want to learn more about *helping verbs*, glide into this site:

www.kyrene.k12.az.us/schools/brises/sunda/verb/1help.htm

We refer to the **main verb + helping verb** (if there is one in the sentence) as the **complete verb**. It's important to determine the complete verb in each sentence so that you can be sure of the correct meaning of the sentence.

> Maria *should prepare* the dinner.

In this sentence, the main verb is *prepare* and the helping verb is *should.* Notice the difference in meaning of this sentence when compared to the following sentence:

> Maria *prepares* the dinner.

Here, you don't have a helping verb. Notice that Maria is actually preparing the dinner. In the first example, you know that someone believes she is supposed to prepare the dinner, but you don't know whether she does.

Let's look at another example:

> Ugo *will do* his homework.

The complete verb *will do* composed of the main verb *do* and the helping verb *will* in this sentence tells you that Ugo has not yet finished his homework. By contrast, in the following sentence:

> Ugo *did* his homework.

You know from the complete verb *did* that Ugo actually finished his homework.

You have learned about ***action verbs***, ***linking verbs***, *and* ***helping verbs***. Not only is it important to describe action and tell more about the subject of the sentence, but also you have to be able to tell your listener or reader when the action or state of being occurred. Let's see how to do this.

VERB TENSES: EXPRESSING PAST, PRESENT, AND FUTURE

You have learned that a ***verb*** expresses an *action* or *state of being*. The **tense** of a verb tells whether that action or the state of being is occurring in the present, occurred in the past, or will occur in the future. The English language uses several tenses, but for now, let's just talk about the three main ones: ***present***, ***past***, and ***future***.

The ***present tense*** describes something that *exists* or *is happening now*. To form the present tense, you usually add an ***–s*** to the verb when the subject is singular. For instance,

> Pham *answers* the question the teacher asks the class.
> Bonita *helps* her mother prepare the dinner.
> Miguel *writes* his vocabulary words in his workbook.
> Maria *throws* the ball.

By comparison, the ***past tense*** describes something that *has existed* or *has already happened*. For most verbs, you can write their past tense form by adding a ***-d*** or ***-ed***.

> Pham *answered* the question that the teacher had asked the class.
> Bonita *helped* her mother prepare the dinner.

All of this seems easy; however, numerous verbs require significant changes in their spelling to form their past tense.

> Miguel *wrote* his vocabulary words in his workbook.
> Maria *threw* the ball to Lucia.

Finally, the ***future tense*** describes something that *will exist* or something that *will happen*. You usually add the *helping verbs* **will** or **shall** to the main verb to show the future tense.

Pham *will answer* the question the teacher asks the class.
Bonita *shall help* her mother prepare the dinner.
Miguel *shall write* his vocabulary words in his notebook.
Maria *will throw* the ball to Lucia.

Surf's up...

Surf into this site for more information about *verb tenses*:

http://www.englishpage.com/verbpage/verbtenseintro.html

If you communicate in the wrong tense, you will confuse your listener or reader. Sometimes that confusion can cause a problem. For instance, if Linda's mother is hurt and needs a doctor, people will react immediately if you say: *Linda's mother* ***needs*** *a doctor*! On the other hand, if you say: *Linda's mother* ***needed*** *a doctor*! They will not do anything.

Now that you can use verbs to express the past, present, and future, let's continue to learn more about verbs. The type of verb and its position in the sentence determine whether the sentence is written in the ***active voice*** or ***passive voice***.

ACTIVE AND PASSIVE VOICE

In the world of grammar, the term ***voice*** refers to how the subject's verb in the sentence performs its job. Consequently, you determine voice by whether the subject *performs* or *receives* the action in the sentence. Let's begin by looking at the ***active voice***.

You say that a verb is in the ***active voice*** when the subject of the sentence is the **performer** of the action. For instance, the following sentence is written in the ***active voice***.

José *kicked* the ball into the goal.

In this sentence, the subject *José* **performs** the action of the sentence *kicked the ball into the goal.*

Let's look at another active voice sentence.

The car *hit* the telephone pole.

You should be able to see that this is an active voice sentence because the subject of the sentence *car* **performs** the action *hit the telephone pole.*

By comparison, a ***passive voice*** sentence's subject **receives** the action of the sentence rather than *performing* the action. Notice how the complete verb in this passive voice sentence consists of a form of the verb "to be" *(was)* and a past participle verb (*kicked*).

The ball *was kicked* into the goal by José.

Notice also that the subject of the sentence *ball* is **receiving**, rather than **performing**, the action of the sentence. Let's look at another passive voice sentence.

The telephone pole *was hit* by the car.

Why is this a passive voice sentence? The answer is because the subject of the sentence *telephone pole* is *receiving* the action of the sentence *hit by the car.* Again, notice the "to be" verb *(was)* combined with the past participle verb *(hit)*.

Surf's up...

Here is a great site for more help identifying the *active voice* and the *passive voice*:

Active voice:
http://www.tarleton.edu/~english/tw/active_voice.html

Passive voice:
http://esl.about.com/library/grammar/blpassive.htm

That ends the discussion of the active voice and the passive voice. Let's take a few minutes to look at some verbs that are commonly misused by people speaking and writing English.

CONFUSING VERB PAIRS

These confusing verbs come in pairs and have similar meanings. Consequently, sometimes writers and speakers choose the wrong one. These verb pairs are: (1) ***lay*** and ***lie***, (2) ***sat*** and ***set***, and (3) ***let*** and ***leave***.

Let's look at the first pair—***lay*** and ***lie***.

Lay and Lie

Lay means to **put** or **place something**.
Lie means to **rest** or **recline**.

Incorrect
Maria needs to *lay* down and rest.

This sentence is written incorrectly because *lay* means to **put** or **place something**. Maria needs to rest.

Correct
Maria needs to *lie* down and rest.

The sentence is now correct because *lie* means to **rest or recline**.

Incorrect
Please *lie* your sleeping bag next to mine.

The writer has chosen the wrong verb because the writer wanted you to place your things in a particular place. By comparison, l*ie* means to **rest** or **recline**.

Correct
Please *lay* your sleeping bag next to mine.

The sentence is now written correctly because the verb *lay* means to **put** or **place something**.

Set and Sit

Set means to **put something somewhere**.
Sit means to **sit down**.

Incorrect
In a few seconds, Ms. Garcia will *set* down in the chair behind her desk.

Ms. Garcia doesn't want to put something somewhere; rather, she merely wants to **sit down** in her chair.

Correct
In a few seconds, Ms. Garcia will *sit* down in the chair behind her desk.

Now this sentence is correctly written because the writer has used the verb *sit*, which describes what Ms. Garcia wants to do.

Incorrect
"Pham, did you *sit* the plates on the table?" asked Carlos.

This sentence is incorrect because things such as plates don't sit down; people and animals sit down.

Correct
Pham, did you *set* the plates on the table?" asked Carlos.

This sentence is correctly written because the writer has used the verb *set*, which means to **put** or **place**. The plates are being placed on the table.

Let and Leave

Let means to **allow**.
Leave means to **allow to remain**.

Incorrect
"Will you *leave* me go with you, Leah?" asked Roman.

This sentence is not correct. *Leave* means to **allow to remain**. Roman is asking Leah for permission or to **be allowed** to go with Leah.

Correct
"Will you *let* me go with you?" asked Roman.

Now you have a correctly written sentence. *Let* means to **allow**.

Incorrect
Juan will *let* your books on Ms. Garcia's desk.

This sentence is incorrect because Juan wants the books **to remain** on Ms. Garcia's desk. *Let* means to **allow**.

Correct
Juan will l*eave* your books on Ms. Garcia's desk.

Here, Juan is allowing the books to remain on Ms. Garcia's desk. Consequently, now the sentence is written correctly.

BRAIN TICKLERS!
Set #3
CONFUSING VERB PAIRS

For each of the sentences below, select the correct ***verb*** from the choices in parenthesis and then write the sentence on the line provided.

EXAMPLE

"Students, will you please (set, sit) in your seats immediately," said Ms. Garcia.

"Students, will you please *sit* in your seats immediately," said Ms. Garcia.

My mother is going to (let, leave) me keep the dog that followed me home from school.

My mother is going to *let* me keep the dog that followed me home from school.

1. The cat wants to (lay, lie) on the sofa with Katie.

____

2. My brother has (sat, set) the table for dinner.

____

3. The dog (sat, set) on the car to keep warm.

____

4. Please, (let, leave) me have a turn.

____

5. I need to (lie, lay) down and rest because I have been working hard all day.

____

6. Before class, Maria (sat, set) her books on her desk.

____

7. Shall I (lie, lay) it over there or right here?

____

8. Because we talk so much, Ms. Nguyen won't (let, leave) me sit next to you in class.

____

9. (Set, Sit) those dishes down over there.

____

10. Please do not allow your dog to (set, sit) on my clean bed.

____

(Answers are on page 252.)

You should now be confident that you could correctly use those pairs of confusing verbs. Now, it's time to learn about words that started out as verbs, but by adding some other words to them or changing their spelling just a bit, they function as other parts of speech. We call these words—***verbals***.

VERBALS

Verbals are words whose roots are verbs but that function as other parts of speech. There are three types of verbals: *gerunds*, *participles*, and *infinitives*. Because they look like verbs, they sometimes confuse even the most experienced writers. Nevertheless, they really are quite easy to understand, so let's take a look at them.

Gerunds

You can form a ***gerund*** by taking a verb and adding *–ing* to the end of it. By doing this, you can use it as a **noun**. Below are some examples of gerunds.

> Good *writing* is the result of a lot of hard work and practice.

As you can see, an *–ing* has been added to the verb *write* to create the gerund *writing*, which is acting as a noun and also as the subject of the sentence.

Let's stop a minute and make sure you don't get confused. Just adding an *–ing* to the end of a verb does not automatically change it to a gerund. The newly formed word is only a gerund if you use it as a **noun** in the sentence. For instance, in our earlier example:

> Good *writing* is the result of a lot of hard work and practice.

Writing is a gerund because it is acting as a **noun** in the sentence. But compare:

> Paulo is *writing* his essay for Ms. Nguyen's class.

In this sentence, *writing* is an **action verb**. It describes the action of the subject *Paulo*.

Now, let's get back to gerunds. Say you have written the following sentence.

> *Dancing* is great exercise, and it's also fun.

Because *dancing* is functioning as a noun in the sentence, you have written the gerund *dancing* by adding an *–ing* to the verb *dance*.

Here's another example:

> Carlos enjoys *learning* different languages.

In the above sentence, the gerund *learning* has been formed by adding an *–ing* to the verb learn. Here, the gerund is the direct object in the sentence.

Participles

A ***participle*** is a verb form that usually ends in *–ing* or *–ed*, but sometimes also *–en* or *–d*. It usually functions as an **adjective**, but occasionally you'll see a participle acting as an **adverb**.

> *Scared,* the kitten ran under the parked car.

The participle *scared* was formed by taking the verb *scare* and adding a *–d*. In this sentence, the participle acts as an adjective, modifying the noun *kitten*. Remember: in the above sentence, *scared* is a participle because it acts as an **adjective**. If the sentence had been:

> Juan *scared* me.

Now, *scared* is a **verb**.

Now let's look at a participle formed by adding *–ing* to a verb.

> The woman *walking* into the classroom is Ms. Garcia.

An *–ing* has been added to the verb *walk* to form the participle *walking*, which is acting as an **adjective** in the sentence by modifying the noun *woman*.

> I saw Carlos *swimming* in the pool.

The participle *swimming* is acting as an **adjective** by modifying the noun *Carlos*. As in the previous example, this participle was formed by adding *–ing* to the verb *swim*.

Because most participles end in *–ing*, they look the same as gerunds. The important difference is that ***participles*** act as *modifiers*, either **adverbs** or **adjectives** while ***gerunds*** function as **nouns**.

> *Laughing* makes you feel good.

In this sentence, *laughing* is a ***gerund*** because it is acting as a **noun** and is the subject of the sentence. By contrast, look at the following sentence:

> A *laughing* person is sometimes annoying.

Here, *laughing* is a ***participle*** formed by adding an *–ing* to the verb *laugh*. It is acting as an **adjective** by modifying the noun *person*.

Infinitives

An ***infinitive*** consists of the basic form of a verb, usually preceded by the preposition *to*. Infinitives can function as **nouns, adjectives**, or **adverbs**. In the following examples, notice how the infinitive *to learn* functions as a noun, or an adjective, or an adverb, depending on how it is used.

> *To learn* requires hard work.

Here the infinitive *to learn* is acting as a **noun** and is the subject of the sentence. But, you have the following sentence.

> Obi had many vocabulary words *to learn.*

In this sentence, the infinitive *to learn* is acting as an **adjective** because it is modifying or describing the noun *vocabulary words*. Finally, you can have

> Tan likes *to learn* about faraway places.

Here, the infinitive *to learn* is acting as an **adverb** because it is modifying or describing the verb *likes*.

Surf's up...

While you surf through cyberspace, you can learn more about *verbals* at this web site:

http://www.uottowa.ca/academic/arts/writcent/hypergrammar/verbals.html

Verbals can be a confusing part of the English language. The following exercise will help you make sure that you can identify them in a sentence.

BRAIN TICKLERS!
Set #4
HEALTHY LIVING

For each of the sentences below, determine whether the underlined word is a ***verb*** or a ***verbal*** (**gerund**, **participle**, or **infinitive**). If the word is a ***verb***, write "verb" on the line provided following each sentence. If the word is a ***verbal***, write the type of verbal that it is on the line provided following each sentence.

EXAMPLE

Healthy *eating* should be a goal for all of us. **gerund**

To improve my health, I am *eating* more fruits and vegetables. **verb**

1. Uninformed, many people eat a poor diet. ________
2. I saw Maria eating an apple at lunch. ________
3. She tries to eat three pieces of fruit every day. ________
4. Substituting a piece of fruit for a bag of potato chips is a good idea. ________
5. Maria said that instead of eating junk food there are many new foods she wants to try. ________
6. Healthy snacking is one of the keys to good nutrition and good health. ________
7. Exercising is another key to good health. ________
8. I try to walk at least a mile every day. ________
9. Watching too much television is not good for you. ________
10. To lose weight is not easy, but sometimes it is necessary. ________

(Answers are on page 252.)

You are now finished with the section on verbs. Now it's time to learn about another important part of speech—***modifiers***.

CHAPTER FOUR

Modifiers

So far, you have learned about three important parts of speech. **Nouns** and **pronouns** name people, places, and things, while **verbs** describe the actions of those people, places, and things. As important as these parts of speech are, they need the help of ***modifiers*** to help them realize their potential and make them effective. Modifiers *describe* nouns, pronouns, and verbs. They give us the interesting and important details about nouns, pronouns, and verbs, and by using modifiers, you will speak and write about your ideas more clearly.

WHAT ARE MODIFIERS?

A ***modifier*** is a word or group of words that describes or limits another word or group of words. There are two main groups of modifiers: ***adjectives*** and ***adverbs***.

ADJECTIVES

An ***adjective*** is a word or group or words that modifies or describes a **noun** or a **pronoun**. Adjectives answer questions such as

- Which one?
- How many?
- What kind of?

The following are some examples of ***adjectives***.

Maria's *blue* backpack is in Ms. Garcia's room.

In the above sentence, *blue* is an adjective modifying the noun backpack. In this sentence, the adjective answers the question: *What kind of?*

All seventh graders enjoy Ms. Garcia's science class.

Here, *all* is the adjective that modifies the noun seventh graders. It answers the question: *How many?*

The *new* student answered the question.

In the above sentence, the adjective *new* identifies the noun student and answers the question: *Which one?*

As with other parts of speech, it is useful to separate the part of speech into groups and learn about each group. You can divide ***adjectives*** into two major groups: ***proper adjectives*** and ***common adjectives***.

PROPER AND COMMON ADJECTIVES

You form ***proper adjectives*** from *proper nouns*. You will recall from Chapter One that a *proper noun* names a specific person, place, thing, idea, animal, quality, or action, and it is capitalized. Consequently, proper adjectives, just like proper nouns, must be capitalized. Below are some examples of proper nouns and proper adjectives. The italicized words below are ***proper adjectives***.

I live in America. This is an *American* flag.
People in Africa are called *Africans*. The Sahara is an *African* desert.
Asians constitute three-fifths of the world population.
Asian food is very healthy.

By contrast, ***common adjectives*** are all the adjectives that aren't proper adjectives. For example,

blue dress
one person
funny hat

Use the following exercise to practice identifying ***common adjectives*** and ***proper adjectives.***

BRAIN TICKLERS!
Set #1
SHARKS

For each of the sentences in this exercise, single underline the ***common adjectives*** and double underline the ***proper adjectives***.

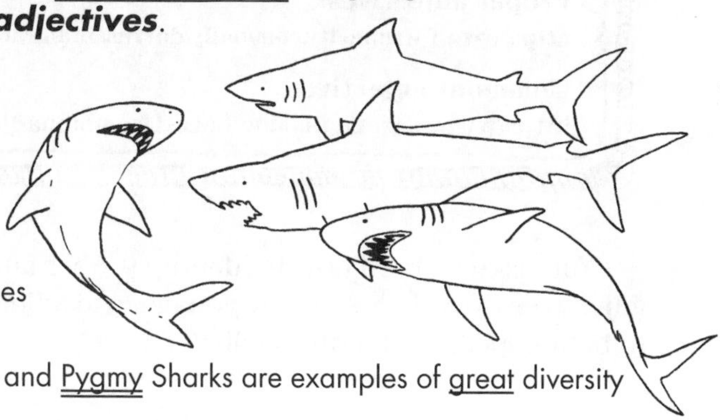

EXAMPLE:

There are 360 species of sharks.

Great White Sharks and Pygmy Sharks are examples of great diversity among sharks.

1. Sharks live an average of twenty-five years.
2. Whale Sharks have three hundred rows of teeth.
3. Adult Great White Sharks grow to lengths of twelve feet to fourteen feet.
4. By contrast, the adult Pygmy Shark is only eleven inches long.
5. Sharks have unusual skeletons.
6. Their skeletons contain zero bones.
7. Instead, the hard skeleton is composed of cartilage.
8. *Cartilage* is tough, elastic tissue.
9. Their well-developed sense of smell helps sharks hunt prey.
10. They can smell one drop of blood dissolved in water.

(Answers are on page 253.)

Surf's up...

Do you want to learn more about *proper adjectives* and *common adjectives*? If you do, then surf into these sites:

Proper adjectives:
http://www.fortunecity.com/bally/durrus/153/gramach21.html

Commons adjectives:
http://www.learnenglish.de/Level1/commonadjectives.htm

You have learned how to identify proper and common adjectives. Now let's see how you can use adjectives to help you to better speak and write English.

IMPROVING YOUR WRITING WITH ADJECTIVES

Adjectives can make your speech and writing more interesting and informative. For instance, suppose you wrote the following sentence:

There is a tree in Juan's backyard. It has branches.

Would someone reading these sentences know much about this tree in Juan's backyard? No, they wouldn't, and because they don't know much about this tree, it's hard for them to be interested in it. How can we make this more informative and interesting? One way is with **adjectives**. By using adjectives, the sentence could become:

There is a *large pecan* tree in Juan's backyard. It has *many broken* and *dead* branches.

Notice that by adding five adjectives (*large*, *pecan*, *many*, *broken*, and *dead*) to the two sentences, you provided your reader much more information about the tree in Juan's backyard.

Let's look at another example. Here is a sentence with no adjectives.

The dog is walking toward the child.

Here, just by adding some adjectives, you created a much different sentence.

The *growling* dog is walking toward the *terrified* child.

Do you notice the difference?

Let's go back to our first example. You could also have written the second sentence as follows:

It has *many broken, dead* branches.

Notice that in this sentence a comma replaced the word *and*. If the adjectives can be separated by the word *and*, then you can also use a comma to separate the adjectives.

Notice the following sentence:

Rex is a *short* and *fat* dog.

This sentence could also be written:

Rex is a *short, fat* dog.

If the adjectives can't be separated by the word *and*, then it isn't necessary to insert a comma between them. For example,

Ricardo has *two younger* sisters.

Use the following exercise below to practice using ***adjectives*** to make your sentences more interesting and informative.

BRAIN TICKLERS!
Set #2
USING OFTEN-USED COMMON ADJECTIVES

This exercise uses some often-used ***common adjectives*** in the English language. Rewrite each of the sentences on the line provided using the adjective in the parenthesis.

EXAMPLE:

The room was filled with students and teachers. (large)

The *large* room was filled with students and teachers.

The clouds warned us of a thunderstorm. (black)

The *black* clouds warned us of a thunderstorm.

1. After everyone sat down, there were empty seats left. (two)

   ____

2. My brother wants to go to school with me. (little)

   ____

3. Alfredo was wearing a shirt. (white)

   ____

4. Has anyone seen my jacket? (brown)

   ____

5. Jorge's father is a man. (kind)

   ____

6. Maria has a cut on her forehead. (small)

   ____

7. I have lost an envelope full of papers. (important)

   ____

8. Clouds filled the sky. (blue)

   ____

9. José is being chased by a dog. (big)

____

10. Mateo wears a jacket every day to school. (different)

____

(Answers are on page 253.)

You have seen how to make your writing more informative and interesting by using adjectives. However, you can go even beyond merely using adjectives to provide information. Let's look at a technique using adjectives that will make your speech and writing flow.

Combining Sentences

Many writers, especially those who are learning the language, use adjectives, but they use them to write short, choppy sentences. The following is an example of this type of writing.

Pham is wearing a *cotton* shirt. Pham is wearing a *blue* shirt.

The writer has used adjectives, but he or she has been repetitive. Because writing is meant to flow, this type of repetitive writing is very uninteresting to those fluent in English. When you have written two or more sentences that contain adjectives that describe the same noun or are predicate adjectives describing the same subject, you should combine them into a single sentence. Because both adjectives describe the same noun **shirt**, you can write:

Pham is wearing a *blue cotton* shirt.

As you saw earlier, sometimes the adjectives can be combined by inserting the word *and* between them. For example, notice the following two sentences:

Pham owns an *old* car.
Pham owns a *noisy* car.

You can combine them into one sentence:

Pham owns an *old* **and** *noisy* car.

In Chapter Three, you learned that words in the predicate following the linking verb sometimes *describe* the subject. When they do this, we call these words **predicate adjectives**. We can also use our combining sentence technique with predicate adjectives. Notice how you could combine the following two sentences:

The girls are *sad*.
The girls are *lonely*.

They can be combined to:

The girls are *sad* **and** *lonely*.

Let's look at another example.

The candy tastes *sweet*.
The candy tastes *fruity*.

You can combine these sentences into the following sentence:

The candy tastes *sweet* **and** *fruity*.

BRAIN TICKLERS!

Set #3

MORE COMMONLY-USED ADJECTIVES

Each of the following exercises contains two or more sentences containing ***adjectives*** that describe the same noun. Combine the sentences into one sentence, and write the new sentence on the line below the exercise.

EXAMPLE:

Mrs. Vu is a *tall* woman.
Mrs. Vu is a *thin* woman.
Mrs. Vu is a *tall, thin* woman.

Mrs. Vu is a *social studies teacher.* Mrs. Vu is a *seventh grade* teacher.
Mrs. Vu is a *seventh grade social studies* teacher.

Mrs. Vu is hard working. Mrs. Vu is conscientious.
Mrs. Vu is *hard working* **and** *conscientious.*

1. Carlos ate two peppers. Carlos ate green peppers.

___

2. Maria is honest. Maria is kind-hearted.

___

3. Katrina is carrying a black purse. Katrina is carrying a little purse.

___

4. Juan's father bought a new car. Juan's father bought a blue car.

___

5. Ugo can juggle three balls. Ugo can juggle round balls. Ugo can juggle green balls.

___

6. The dirt is brown. The dirt is cold.

___

7. Armando's computer is small. Armando's computer is light.

___

8. Julio is creative. Julio is intelligent.

___

9. At the circus, we saw six bears. At the circus, we saw black bears.

___

10. Alexis sent her grandmother three letters. Alexis sent her grandmother short letters.

___

(Answers are on page 253.)

Adjective Variety

Another problem students learning a new language encounter when using adjectives is they sometimes use the same adjectives throughout their writing. Let's look at the following paragraph.

The **big** man walked into the **big** house. He sat in a **big** chair at a **big** table. Before him was a **big** meal, which would be enough to satisfy his **big** appetite.

Notice that the writer used the adjective **big** six times. Did you notice how boring the paragraph was? You can avoid this type of writing by learning some new words that have a similar meaning to the adjective you have repetitiously used. These words with similar meanings are called ***synonyms***. The following are some commonly used adjectives and below them are some of the synonyms for these adjectives.

Big	**Pretty**	**Fast**	**Important**
large	attractive	sudden	significant
huge	beautiful	speedy	vital
considerable	cute	swift	central
bulky	nice-looking	high-speed	critical
extensive	good-looking	immediate	key
spacious	gorgeous	prompt	main

Small	**New**	**Old**	**Slow**
little	fresh	ancient	sluggish
tiny	innovative	aged	deliberate
petite	latest	elderly	leisurely
undersized	inexperienced	experienced	lethargic
minor	original	antique	easygoing
miniature	modern	early	unhurried

Let's take our earlier paragraph and substitute our synonyms for the adjective *big*.

The **bulky** man walked into the **spacious** house. He sat in a **big** chair at an **extensive** table. Before him was a **huge** meal, which would be enough to satisfy his **considerable** appetite.

Where can you find synonyms for words such as adjectives? The answer is in a book called a **thesaurus**. A thesaurus is similar to a dictionary in that words in it are listed in alphabetical order. By contrast, rather than listing definitions, it lists words that mean the same as the word of interest (*synonyms*) and words that are opposite in meaning (*antonyms*).

Use the following exercise to practice finding ***synonyms*** for commonly used adjectives.

BRAIN TICKLERS!
Set #4
THE CONSTITUTION OF THE UNITED STATES

For each of the sentences below, use a thesaurus and find a ***synonym*** for the underlined **adjective**. Rewrite the sentence with the new adjective on the line provided below.

EXAMPLE:

The Constitution of the United States is the highest law of the United States; whereas the constitutions of the states are their highest laws.

The Constitution of the United States is the *primary* law in the United States; whereas the constitutions of the states are their highest laws.

1. The Constitution created three independent branches of government that had certain responsibilities and had to work together if the government was to function.

____

2. Written in 1787, the Constitution is an old document.

____

3. The United States was a new country when the Constitution was written.

____

4. Writing the Constitution was a difficult task.

____

5. At the time the Constitution was being written, the United States had an insufficient government.

____

6. The Framers wanted to meet and find a new way of running the country.

___

7. The well-known meeting was called the Constitutional Convention.

___

8. The original Constitution did not specifically mention personal rights.

___

9. Because the first ten amendments to the Constitution set out personal rights, these first ten amendments are important amendments.

___

10. These early amendments are called the Bill of Rights.

___

(Some possible answers are on page 254.)

You've learned how to work with common adjectives and proper adjectives. Now, let's look at a few other types of adjectives.

ARTICLES

Another important group of adjectives is known as ***articles***. Articles are special types of adjectives that *point* to nouns. Consequently, when you use an article, it must always appear before the noun. You can divide articles into two groups: ***indefinite articles*** and ***definite articles***.

An ***indefinite article*** points to any one of a group of people or things without pointing to a specific person or thing. The two indefinite articles are:

an Used before nouns that begin with a vowel.
Vowels are the letters: *a*, *e*, *i*, *o*, *u*, and *y* (sometimes)

Ugo ate *an* apple and then *an* orange.
An eagle flew past the tourists.

a Used before nouns that begin with a consonant.
Consonants are all the letters that are not vowels.

Carlos gave me *a* pencil and *a* piece of paper.
Roman was photographing *a* bird sitting on *a* tree branch.

Incorrect
Roman photographed *an* dog swimming in the water.

This sentence is incorrectly written because the indefinite article *an* is being used to point to the noun **dog**. However, since *dog* starts with a consonant, the indefinite article *a* should be used.

Correct
Roman photographed *a* dog swimming in the water.

This sentence is now correctly written because the indefinite article *a* is used before the noun **dog**.

A ***definite article*** points to a specific thing or person within a group. There is only one definite article in the English language—**the**. The word **the** is also the most commonly used word in the English language.

Pham walked into *the* room and shut *the* window I had opened.
The book I am reading is about astronauts.

Incorrect
Ms. Garcia asked Pham to turn in *a* homework that was due.

This sentence is incorrectly written because the sentence is referring to a specific piece of homework—the homework that was due. Therefore, the writer needs to use the definite article *the* to point to the **homework**.

Correct
Ms. Garcia asked Pham to turn in *the* homework that was due.

This sentence is now correctly written because the writer is using the definite article *the* to point to the noun **homework**.

BRAIN TICKLERS!
Set #5
Eagles

For each of the sentences below, select the correct ***article(s)*** and write the article on the line(s) provided at the end of the sentence.

EXAMPLE:

Bald eagles are (a, an) symbol of beauty and power.
a____

(A, The) bald eagle population in the United States is beginning to increase. **The**____

1. (The, An) bald eagle is our national bird. ______
2. The bald eagle is not bald, but rather has (a, an) group of white feathers on top of its head. ______
3. At one time in the English language, (an, the) word "bald" meant "white." ______
4. Bald eagles are found over most of (an, the) North American continent. ______
5. About half of (a, the) 70,000 bald eagles live in Alaska. ______
6. Lots of salmon live in (a, the) rivers of Alaska. ______
7. Salmon are (a, an) important part of (a, an) eagle's diet. ______, ______
8. (A, An) eagle will also eat other kinds of fish. ______
9. (A, An) female bald eagle grows to a height of 36 inches, slightly larger than the male. ______
10. Eagles have (a, an) wingspan of 80 to 90 inches. ______

(Answers are on page 254.)

Surf's up...

Here's a good site providing additional information about *articles*:

http://www.unc.edu/depts/wcweb/handouts/articles.html

Now that you have learned about articles, let's look at another important group of adjectives—***demonstrative adjectives***.

DEMONSTRATIVE ADJECTIVES

A ***demonstrative adjective*** points out a particular person or thing and answers the question *which one?* or *which ones?* Examples of demonstrative adjectives are **this**, **these**, **that**, **those**.

This and **these** point out people or things nearby in time or distance. **That** and **those** point out people or things farther away in time or distance. Use **these** and **those** with plural nouns. Use **this** and **that** with singular nouns.

If you give me *that* magazine on the table in the other room, I'll give you *this* book.

I think *these* grapes are much sweeter than *those* grapes we ate at Pham's house.

I like *this* sweater better than *those* jackets over there.

Try one of *these* cookies and a piece of *this* pie.

Incorrect

That book in my hand is one of my favorites.

This sentence is incorrectly written because the noun that is modified **book** is nearby and singular. Therefore, this sentence requires you to use the demonstrative adjective *this*, which modifies nouns that are nearby and singular.

Correct
This book in my hand is one of my favorites.

The sentence is now correct because the demonstrative adjective *this* is modifying the noun **book**.

Incorrect
These apple I ate yesterday was very sweet tasting.

This sentence is incorrectly written because the noun **apple** modified by the demonstrative adjective *these* is singular and farther away in time. To write this sentence properly, use the demonstrative adjective *that*, which modifies singular nouns that are farther away in time.

Correct
That apple I ate yesterday was very sweet tasting.

The sentence is now correct because the writer used the demonstrative adjective *that*, which is needed to modify nouns that are singular and farther away in time.

Incorrect
These books in Ms. Garcia's room down the hall belong to Ugo.

The noun **books** is modified by the demonstrative adjective *these*, which is plural and farther away in distance; therefore, this sentence is incorrectly written. The demonstrative adjective *these* should be used to modify nouns that are plural and nearby in distance.

Correct
Those books in Ms. Garcia's room down the hall belong to Ugo.

The sentence is now correctly written because the demonstrative adjective *those* is modifying the noun that is plural and farther away in distance.

IMPORTANT!

Don't be confused by the words *this*, *that*, *these*, and *those*. As you learned in Chapter Two, when these words replace nouns, they are *demonstrative pronouns*. By contrast, as you have seen in this section, when you write *this*, *that*, *these*, and *those* before nouns (*this* coat, *that* man, *these* people), those words are *demonstrative adjectives*.

BRAIN TICKLERS!
Set #6
WRITING WITH DEMONSTRATIVE ADJECTIVES

For each of the sentences below, select the correct ***demonstrative adjective*** from the choices in the parenthesis. Write your answer on the line provided to the right of the sentence.

EXAMPLE:

I'm going to eat (those, these) pancakes sitting on my plate. **these**

1. (This, That) man sitting next to me is my father. _______
2. (Those, These) men over there are my uncles. _______
3. Uncle Tito gave me (this, that) jacket I'm wearing. _______
4. He also gave me (this, those) shoes sitting by the door. _______
5. (That, This) woman who just left here was my Aunt Estelle. _______
6. I am going to learn (this, these) vocabulary words on this worksheet. _______

7. What does (this, those) word mean? _______
8. Try one of (these, that) cookies I made. _______
9. Let me finish (this, that) cookie I'm eating now. _______
10. (Those, These) cookies on that plate over there are for my uncles. _______

(Answers are on page 255.)

Surf's up...

Glide into this site to learn more about *demonstrative adjectives*.

http://www.arts.uottowa.ca/writcent/hypergrammar/adjective.html

You should be familiar with demonstrative adjectives. Now, it's time to learn about another group of important adjectives—***indefinite adjectives.***

INDEFINITE ADJECTIVES

Indefinite adjectives describe general, rather than specific, qualities. Examples of indefinite adjectives include **all**, **another**, **any**, **both**, **each**, **either**, **few**, **many**, **more**, **most**, **other**, **several**, and **some**.

> *Some* students enjoy writing stories.
>
> *Each* student should try to find the best way he or she learns to read and write English.
>
> *Many* languages are more difficult to learn than English is.
>
> *Most* students recognize the importance of writing clearly.
>
> I gave the same instructions to *both* girls.

Use the following exercise to help you identify ***indefinite adjectives.***

BRAIN TICKLERS!
Set #7
THE FIRST AMERICANS

For each of the sentences below, underline the ***indefinite adjectives***. On the line following the sentence, write a new sentence by substituting a different ***indefinite adjective*** (**all**, **another**, **any**, **both**, **each**, **either**, **few**, **many**, **more**, **most**, **other**, **several**, **some**) for the ***indefinite adjective*** that you underlined.

Notice how doing this changes the meaning of the sentence.

EXAMPLE:

Some scientists believe that many people first came to America by crossing the Bering Strait from Asia.

Many scientists believe that **most** people first came to America by crossing the Bering Strait from Asia.

1. Their *migration* or journey probably first started over 11,000 years ago, and later more migrants followed.

   ____

2. Christopher Columbus first applied the name "Indian" to all Native Americans he encountered.

   ____

3. He believed that each island he visited was part of the East Indies of Asia.

   ____

4. Many tribes of Native Americans lived throughout North America.

   ____

5. Each tribe had its special traditions and culture.

____

6. One of the many North American tribes is the Apaches.

____

7. As did most Native Americans, the Apaches believed that everything in nature had special powers.

____

8. Both Apaches and the Navajos lived in the Southwest.

____

9. There were several Iroquois tribes.

____

10. A few Iroquois tribes include the Mohawk, the Oneida, and the Seneca.

____

(Some possible answers are on page 255.)

Surf's up...

Surf into this site for more information about *indefinite adjectives*.

http://www.uottawa.ca/academic/arts/writcent/hypergrammar/adjective.html

PRONOUNS AS ADJECTIVES

In Chapter Two, you learned about pronouns and how you could use them to replace nouns. In the following example, notice how the pronoun *her* is used in place of the noun **Ms. Garcia**.

Carlos gave his homework to **Ms. Garcia**.

Carlos gave his homework to **her**.

By contrast, in the following sentence a pronoun is not used to replace a noun, but rather to show possession or ownership.

Ms. Garcia left *her* notebook in the classroom.

The pronoun *her* modifies the noun **notebook**. You know the notebook belongs to Ms. Garcia and that she left it in the classroom.

I need *your* textbook to finish *my* homework.

The first italicized pronoun *your* modifies the noun **textbook**, and the second italicized pronoun *my* modifies the noun **homework**. Because of these pronoun adjectives, you now know that my homework is unfinished, and I need your textbook to finish it.

Ms. Garcia showed us photographs of *her* children.

The pronoun *her* modifies the noun **children**. The writer has made you aware that Ms. Garcia has children.

The following exercise will provide you with some practice identifying ***pronoun adjectives***.

BRAIN TICKLERS!
Set #8
EATING A NUTRITIOUS BREAKFAST

For each of the sentences below, underline the ***pronoun adjective***. On the line at the end of the sentence, write the noun the adjective is modifying.

EXAMPLE:

My experience shows that nourishing food not only makes a child healthier, but also makes him or her a better student. **experience**

Paying attention to your eating habits is very important. **habits**

1. The type of food we eat for our breakfast is extremely important. _______
2. Juan told us that usually his breakfast was a bowl of cereal and a glass of orange juice. _______
3. A good breakfast will keep your body from getting hungry in the morning. _______

4. Ugo said that sometimes his breakfast is a doughnut. _______
5. He said his hunger returns well before lunchtime. _______
6. What can we learn from his experience? _______
7. If I eat just a doughnut for breakfast, my energy will last only about 40 minutes. _______
8. Your energy will be gone by the time school starts. _______
9. We need our energy to pay attention and learn. _______
10. Your breakfast can help make you a good student. _______

(Answers are on page 256.)

You have learned about some important groups of adjectives and how they help you speak and write better by describing nouns and pronouns. Now it's time to learn about the other main category of modifiers—***adverbs.***

ADVERBS

An ***adverb*** modifies **verbs**, other **adverbs**, and **adjectives**. Adverbs can also modify an entire sentence or a clause. Adverbs answer questions such as

- When?
- Where?
- How?
- How much?
- Why?

Let's look at some adverbs in the following sentences.

The grass was *very* **wet**.

In this sentence, the adverb *very* modifies the predicate adjective **wet**. The adverb answers the question, *how much*?

The students started cheering *quite* **suddenly**.

The adverb *quite* modifies another adverb **suddenly**. The adverb answers the question, *when*? The next sentence also answers the question, *when*?

Pham **called** me on the telephone *yesterday*.

The adverb *yesterday* modifies the verb **called** and answers the question, *when*?

Paulo **laughed** *loudly*.

The adverb *loudly* modifies the verb **laughed**. The adverb answers the question, *how*?

Ugo **ran** *here*.

The adverb *here* modifies the verb **ran**. The adverb answers the question, *where*?

Quickly, **Pham walks to the front of the classroom**.

The adverb *quickly* modifies the verb **walks** but also the entire rest of the sentence, and answers the question, *how*?

Take some time and use the following exercise to help you make sure that you can identify ***adverbs***.

BRAIN TICKLERS!

Set #9

GEEKCORPS: BRINGING TECHNOLOGY TO EVERYONE

For each of the sentences below, underline the ***adverb*** or ***adverbs*** in the sentence.

EXAMPLE

Geekcorps consists of very intelligent and technically sophisticated people who want to share their knowledge with people in underdeveloped countries.

1. The Geekcorps is very similar to the Peace Corps in its goal to help the less fortunate people of the world.
2. It is a nonprofit organization that places volunteers in developing nations badly needing modern technology.
3. Their members usually volunteer after they graduate from college or have been working for a few years.
4. Typically, the volunteers have recently earned engineering or computer science degrees.
5. Many of the volunteers have highly specialized skills learned from working in the communication and computer industries.
6. Millions of people living in impoverished countries are completely lacking any type of modern communication and information systems.
7. Each day, this lack of relatively simple technology puts them further behind the citizens of rapidly developing countries.

8. This daily increasing gap significantly contributes to their poverty.
9. Currently, Geekcorps is seeking extremely motivated volunteers to work in Africa.
10. Africa has been nearly forgotten by the more advanced nations of the world.

(Answers are on page 256.)

Surf's up...

Do you want to read more about *adverbs*? The following site will provide more information about them.

http://web2.uvcs.uvic.ca/elc/studyzone/410/grammar/adverb.htm

RECOGNIZING ADJECTIVES AND ADVERBS

Recognizing adjectives and adverbs can be confusing at times. Adverbs often end in ***–ly***, but a few adjectives end in ***–ly***. For instance, notice the following adjectives: *lively* child, *hilly* area, and *friendly* dog.

The lesson to be learned from these examples is that when determining whether a word is an adjective or an adverb, look not at the word itself but what the word **describes** or modifies. Remember: ***Adjectives*** describe **nouns** and **pronouns**. By contrast, ***adverbs*** modify **verbs**, **adjectives**, and other **adverbs**.

To speak and write English correctly, you must use adjectives and adverbs properly. Let's look at the following examples.

Incorrect
My mother told my brother to please drive *careful.*

This sentence is incorrectly written because the word *careful* is meant to modify the verb **drive**. However, *careful* is an adjective. Consequently, the writer needs to use the adverb *carefully.*

Correct
My mother told my brother to please drive *carefully.*

The sentence is now written correctly because the adverb *carefully* is modifying the verb **drive**.

Incorrect
My neighborhood is very *quietly.*

This sentence is incorrectly written because the word *quietly* is meant to modify the noun **neighborhood**. Consequently, the writer needs to use the adjective *quiet*, rather than the adverb *quietly.*

Correct
My neighborhood is very *quiet.*

The sentence is now correctly written because the adjective *quiet* is modifying the noun **neighborhood**.

Sentences using *linking verbs* require adjectives because linking verbs describe nouns, rather than express action.

Incorrect
My dog smells *badly* because a skunk sprayed him.

This sentence is incorrectly written because the sentence uses the linking verb *smells*, which describes the noun **dog**. Consequently, the writer needs to use an adjective.

Correct
My dog smells *bad* because a skunk sprayed him.

Now the sentence is correctly written because the writer has used the adjective *bad*.

The Good and Well Problem

Good is always an ***adjective***, and so you must use it when describing a noun or a pronoun. Use *well* as an ***adverb*** meaning to *perform capably*. *Well*, therefore, describes verbs, other adverbs, or adjectives.

Max is a *good* dog. He behaves *well*.

Notice how the adjective *good* modifies the noun **dog**, and how the adverb *well* modifies the verb **behaves**.

We had a *good* day because everything went *well*.

In this sentence, the adjective *good* modifies the noun **day**, and the adverb *well* modifies the verb **went**.

If someone asks you, "How do you feel?" How would you answer? Many people will incorrectly say, "I feel good." However, you know now that good is an *adjective*, and so, the correct response is, "I feel well."

The following exercise will provide you with practice determining whether your writing requires an ***adjective*** or an ***adverb***.

BRAIN TICKLERS!
Set #10
CELEBRATIONS AROUND THE WORLD

For each of the sentences below, select the correct ***adjective*** or ***adverb*** from the choices in the parentheses. Write your answer on the line provided at the end of the sentence.

EXAMPLE:

Many celebrations and traditions contribute to the (rich, richly) diversity of the United States. **rich**

Many of these celebrations include (wonderful, wonderfully) ornate clothing. **wonderfully**

1. Some of the more (popular, popularly) celebrations are Christmas, Hanukkah, Juneteenth, Cinco de Mayo, Ramadan, and the Chinese New Year. _______
2. In many regions of the United States, the (beautiful, beautifully) ritual of *Las Posadas* is kept up. _______
3. This is a ritual procession and play representing Mary and Joseph's (unsuccessful, unsuccessfully) search for a room. _______

4. Hanukkah is a Jewish holiday, also (common, commonly) referred to as the Festival of Lights. _______
5. The (actual, actually) celebration of Hanukkah lasts for eight days. _______
6. "Hanukkah" is a Hebrew word that (literal, literally) translated means "dedication." _______
7. Juneteenth (symbolic, symbolically) marks the end of slavery in the United States. _______
8. On June 19, 1865, Major General Granger landed in Galveston, Texas, and (excited, excitedly) announced the war was over. _______
9. The now (wide, widely) celebrated holiday of Cinco de Mayo commemorates the victory of the Mexicans over the French army at The Battle of Puebla in 1862. _______
10. The Chinese New Year is (wide, widely) celebrated throughout the world, especially in China, Japan, Korea, and Vietnam. _______

(Answers are on page 256.)

DEGREES OF ADJECTIVES AND ADVERBS

There are three ***degrees*** of adjectives and adverbs: **positive**, **comparative**, and **superlative**. Use the **positive degree** when you are describing a single person, action, or thing. By contrast, use the **comparative degree** when you are comparing two people, things, or actions. Finally, use the **superlative degree** when you are comparing more than two people, things, or actions.

Most one-syllable and some two-syllable adjectives form the comparative and superlative degrees by adding ***–er*** or ***–est***. For example,

Positive degree	Comparative degree	Superlative degree
sweet	sweeter	sweetest
happy	happier	happiest

I am eating a *sweet* piece of candy.
I am now eating the *sweeter* of the two pieces of candy.
This is the *sweetest* piece of candy I have ever eaten!

If an adjective has more than two syllables, it usually forms the comparative and superlative degrees by preceding the positive degree with the words *more* and *most.* Notice the following example:

Positive degree	Comparative degree	Superlative degree
intelligent	more intelligent	most intelligent
extensive	more extensive	most extensive

The dog is an *intelligent* animal.
A chimpanzee is *more intelligent* than a dog.
A whale may be the *most intelligent* of all animals.

There are a few adjectives that are exceptions to these rules. For example,

Positive degree	Comparative degree	Superlative degree
good	better	best
bad	worse	worst

My mom made us a *good* lunch.
My mom made us a *better* lunch yesterday.
My mom made us the *best* lunch ever.

By comparison, most adverbs form the comparative and superlative forms by using *more* and *most.* For instance,

Positive degree	Comparative degree	Superlative degree
easily	more easily	most easily
slowly	more slowly	most slowly

Roman *easily* ran the distance. **(positive degree)**
Roman ran the distance *more easily* than Pham. **(comparative degree)**
Of the runners, Roman ran the distance *most easily.* **(superlative degree)**

As with adjectives, there are a few adverbs that are exceptions to this rule. For example,

Positive degree	Comparative degree	Superlative degree
hard	harder	hardest
fast	faster	fastest
soon	sooner	soonest

I ran *fast.* **(positive degree)**
Carlos ran *faster* than I did. **(comparative degree)**
Luis ran *fastest* of all the runners. **(superlative degree)**

Now it's your turn to try your skill in working with ***degrees*** of adjectives and adverbs.

BRAIN TICKLERS!
Set #11
A DAY AT THE BEACH

For each of the sentences below, select the correct ***degree*** of the adjective or adverb. Write your answer on the line at the end of the sentence.

EXAMPLE:

We (thorough, thoroughly) searched the beach for starfish. **thoroughly**

Of all the people searching, Luis was the (most thorough, thoroughest). **most thorough**

1. I (real, really) enjoy going to the beach. _______
2. We saw (more, most) fish jumping out of the water than we did last time. _______
3. While we were watching, one (sudden, suddenly) jumped out of the water. _______
4. Unfortunately, it was the (hotter, hottest) day of the year. _______

5. The sun was shining (bright, brightly). _______
6. We were (careful, carefully) not to get sunburned. _______
7. I don't know which is (worse, worst), to be too hot or to be too cold. _______
8. The waves are (highly, higher) than they were this morning. _______
9. I always have a (good, well) time at the beach. _______
10. Of all the places I go, I have the (more, most) fun at the beach. _______

(Answers are on page 256.)

Surf's up...

If you feel you need to know more about *adjectives* and *adverbs*, try this site:

Adjectives:

http://arts.uottowa.ca/writcen/hypergrammar/adjective.html

Adverbs:

http://arts.uottowa.ca/writcen/hypercgrammar/adjective.html

Now that you have learned about modifiers, its time to learn about another important part of speech—***prepositions*.**

CHAPTER FIVE

Prepositions

You've learned about some pretty important parts of speech: nouns, pronouns, verbs, and modifiers. This chapter will talk about another important part of speech—***prepositions***. The hardest thing about prepositions is describing what they do. Basically, prepositions allow nouns that are not directly associated with the verb of the sentence to have a part in the sentence. Many English teachers will say prepositions help to "glue" nouns to the sentence.

WHAT ARE PREPOSITIONS?

A ***preposition*** is a word that shows the relationship between a noun or pronoun and another noun or pronoun.

José's dog is *under* the table.

How do you recognize a preposition? It's sometimes not easy. Prepositions aren't as obvious as nouns or verbs. Nouns name people, places, and things, and verbs describe action or state of being. So how do you identify prepositions? The answer is that you should look for a word that establishes a relationship between two nouns in the sentence. For example in the sentence above, what is the relationship between **José's dog** and the **table**? The preposition *under* describes that relationship—the dog is under the table.

My math class is *after* my social studies class.

In this sentence, the preposition *after* describes the relationship, in time, between the **math class** and the **social studies class**—that is, one follows the other in time. Let's look at one more example:

The hawk flew *across* the cloudless sky.

Here, the preposition *across* describes the relationship between the **hawk** and the **sky**—it flew across it.

SIMPLE AND COMPOUND PREPOSITIONS

There are two major groups of prepositions: ***simple prepositions*** and ***compound prepositions***.

Simple Prepositions

The English language has approximately seventy ***simple prepositions***. They are called **simple** because they are formed from simple words, most of which have two syllables. Below is a list of some of these ***simple prepositions***.

about	above	across	after	against
along	among	around	at	before
behind	below	beside	between	beyond
by	concerning	down	during	except
for	in	into	like	of
off	on	onto	out	over
past	since	through	throughout	to
toward	under	up	upon	which
within	without			

Notice that many of these words such as *on*, *off*, *behind*, and *under* show a relationship concerning **location**.

The textbook is *on* the desk.
Carla fell *off* her bicycle.
Ramon hid *behind* the post.
Pham put his homework *under* his backpack.
The moth moved *toward* the light.
Carlos jumped *into* the water.

By contrast, some of the prepositions such as *before* and *after* show a **time** relationship.

Ms. Garcia arrived *after* Mr. Vu.
They arrived *before* I did.
We go to school *during* the day.

Finally, others show **basic relationships** (*of*, *for*, *to*, and *with*).

The body *of* a tiger is very muscular.
Bonita made a cake *for* her friend.
Both of the girls are going *to* the party.
I am going *with* my cousin.

Surf's up...

If you want to learn more about *simple prepositions*, glide into this site:

http://simple.wikipedia.ord/wiki/Preposition

Now that you are familiar with simple prepositions, let's look at another major group of prepositions—***compound prepositions***.

Compound Prepositions

As opposed to simple prepositions, ***compound prepositions*** are two or three words in length. The following are some examples of compound prepositions: *according to*, *because of*, *in front of*, *instead of*, *in favor of*, *in spite of*, *next to*, *prior to*, *similar to*, *subsequent to*.

Juan's car is parked *in front of* the store.

Notice how the compound preposition *in front of* describes the relationship between **Juan's car** and the **store**.

Ugo sat *next to* Marta at the pep rally.

In the above sentence, the compound preposition *next to* describes where **Ugo** sat with relation to **Marta**.

We were late *because of* the heavy traffic.

In this last example, the compound preposition *because of* shows the relationship between the **lateness** and the **heavy traffic**.

Use the following exercise to give yourself some practice identifying and writing ***compound prepositions***.

BRAIN TICKLERS!

Set #1

USING COMPOUND PREPOSITIONS

in front of	across from	next to	in place of
out of	because of	instead of	in favor of
prior to	similar to		

For each of the sentences below, select one of the ***compound prepositions*** from the above list and write the sentence on the line provided.

EXAMPLE:

I am going to sit ______ Marta at the movie.

I am going to sit *next to* Marta at the movie.

1. My locker is _______ Ms. Garcia's room.

   ____

2. Mr. Vu arrived _______ the opening of the school play.

   ____

3. I would like to go to the zoo _______ the aquarium.

   ____

4. The amazing fish jumped _______ the water!

   ____

5. My uncle parked his truck _______ my house.

   ____

6. The class voted _______ going on a field trip.

   ____

7. We had to leave early _______ the threatening storm clouds.

   ____

8. The taste of this meat is _______ chicken.

____

9. Although he is not as good a player, Ricardo is playing _______ Juan because Juan is injured.

____

10. Who is that standing _______ you?

____

(Answers are on page 257.)

You have studied the two major groups of prepositions, and now it is time to see how they function within a sentence. To do that, let's look at ***prepositional phrases***.

PREPOSITIONAL PHRASES

A ***prepositional phrase*** is a group of words that begins with a **preposition** and ends with a **noun** or **pronoun**. This ending noun or pronoun is called the **object of the preposition**. Below are some examples of prepositional phrases. The preposition is *italicized* and the object of the preposition is underlined.

to the limit
over the top
by the side
inside the house
next to me

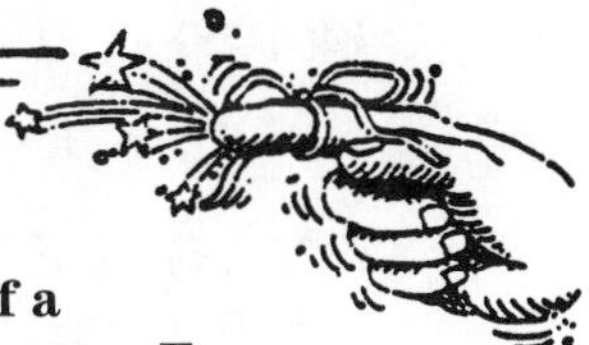

IMPORTANT!

Whenever a *pronoun* serves as the object of a preposition, it must appear in the objective case. For example: next to *me*.

The following exercise will help you to make sure that you can identify ***prepositional phrases***.

BRAIN TICKLERS!
Set #2
GEORGE WASHINGTON AS OUR FIRST PRESIDENT

For each of the sentences below, identify and underline the ***prepositional phrase(s).***

EXAMPLE:

After serving as the Constitutional Convention's president, George Washington was declared our first president.

1. Washington was declared our first president in 1789.
2. As president, he served for two terms.
3. Each term lasted for four years.
4. His presidency lasted until the year 1796.
5. During his presidency, the Bill of Rights became law on December 15, 1791.
6. He made many difficult decisions over the years.
7. He returned to Mount Vernon after his presidency.
8. He went on a horseback ride on December 12, 1799.
9. The weather was cold and snowy during his ride.
10. He became sick because of his ride and died on December 14, 1799.

(Answers are on page 257.)

Surf's up...

To learn more about *prepositional phrases*, check out this site:

http://esl.about.com/b/a/155624.htm

You should feel confident that you could identify a prepositional phrase. Now, let's learn a little more about them.

PREPOSITIONAL PHRASES AS MODIFIERS

Prepositional Phrases as Adjectives

A prepositional phrase can act as an **adjective**. That means, a prepositional phrase can modify a **noun** or a **pronoun**. For instance,

The **woman** *on the hill* is Yolanda.

The prepositional phrase *on the hill* describes or modifies the noun **woman**.

The **story** *about space travel* is exciting.

In the above sentence, the prepositional phrase *about space travel* modifies the noun **story**.

He is *in the classroom.*

Here, the prepositional phrase *in the classroom* describes the pronoun **he**.

Prepositional Phrases as Adverbs

A prepositional phrase can also act as an **adverb**. That is, the prepositional phrase can modify or describe a verb or another other adverb.

The children **shouted** *in loud voices.*

Here, the prepositional phrase *in loud voices* modifies the verb **shouted**.

Pham and Ugo **hid** *behind the wall.*

In the above sentence, the prepositional phrase *behind the wall* modifies the verb **hid**.

The man **talking** *on the telephone* is my father.

Here, the prepositional phrase *on the telephone* modifies the verb **talking**.

You should be comfortable identifying prepositions and prepositional phrases, as well as, understanding the function they perform in the sentence. The next section will help you to identify and avoid some common errors using prepositions in speaking and writing English.

COMMON PREPOSITION ERRORS

Adding Unnecessary Simple Prepositions

Many speakers and writers use simple prepositions unnecessarily. By doing so, they make their speech or writing wordy and confusing.

Incorrect
Ms. Garcia asked, "Where have you been *at*?"

In the sentence above, the simple preposition is unnecessary. The sentence is clear without it.

Correct
Ms. Garcia asked, "Where have you been?"

The sentence is now correctly written because the unnecessary simple preposition *at* has been eliminated.

Incorrect
Where is Carlos going *to*?

This sentence is incorrectly written because the writer has added the unnecessary simple preposition *to* to the end of the sentence.

Correct
Where is Carlos going?

The sentence reads clearly without writing the simple preposition *to* at the end of the sentence.

Using Two Prepositions Where Only One Is Needed

You have seen how writers sometimes make the mistake of using an unnecessary simple preposition in sentences. Similarly, a related error occurs when writers use two prepositions when only one is needed.

> Incorrect
> Don't go *near to* the growling dog.

In the above sentence, the simple preposition *to* isn't needed to make the sentence read clearly. Rather, the preposition just creates unnecessary wordiness.

> Correct
> Don't go *near* the growling dog.

This sentence is now correctly written because the writer has eliminated the unnecessary simple preposition *to*.

> Incorrect
> The cat jumped *off of* the sofa.

This sentence is incorrectly written because it contains the unnecessary simple preposition *of*.

> Correct
> The cat jumped *off* the sofa.

The above sentence is now written correctly because the writer has eliminated the unnecessary simple preposition *of*.

Before you read about one more common error associated with prepositions, let's stop here and use the following exercise to make sure you can identify the errors involving ***unnecessary simple prepositions***.

BRAIN TICKLERS!
Set #3
POLAR BEARS

For each of the sentences below, underline the ***unnecessary simple preposition(s).***

EXAMPLE:

The adult male polar bear is the largest among of the bear family.

The adult male polar bear is the largest *of* the polar bear family.

1. The adult male weighs in between 800 and 1200 pounds.
2. When born, most polar bears weigh like under a pound.
3. The polar bears live on the ice during over the winter and spring.
4. Seals hunt for the fish living in under the water beneath the ice.
5. Polar bears live off of seal meat.
6. They hunt seals near to the ice's edge.
7. The bears look for the seals' breathing holes around in the ice.
8. Polar bears need ice to survive on.
9. Unfortunately, the ice is melting off.
10. If this ice cap melting continues on, the entire bear species could go extinct.

(Answers are on page 257.)

Now let's look at the final error speakers and writers commonly make with prepositions—using ***compound prepositional phrases.***

Avoid Using Compound Prepositional Phrases

A ***compound prepositional phrase*** is a series of prepositional phrases that act like a single preposition. Many writers ignore simple, powerful prepositions such as *on* and *of*. Instead, they select a wordy compound prepositional phrase because they think this makes the writing style appear more sophisticated. However, the opposite is true because it is the lazy writer who uses the compound prepositional phrase rather than taking the time to select the proper verb and preposition.

Below are some common compound prepositional phrases. As you read them, notice how they are formed.

> with regard to = with regard + to
> with respect to = with respect + to
> in reference to = in reference + to

As you can see, a ***compound prepositional phrase*** begins with a complete prepositional phrase. However, it is a prepositional phrase that cannot stand by itself so it must combine forces with another preposition just to link the noun to the sentence. Consequently, you fill the page with more words than you need to express your ideas. Avoid using compound prepositional phrases by changing any that you may have written to simple prepositions or eliminating the entire compound prepositional phrase. Below are some examples demonstrating how some wordy compound prepositions can be reduced to single-word prepositions.

> <u>Incorrect</u>
> *In order to* write more concisely, eliminate compound prepositional phrases.

This sentence is incorrectly written because the writer has used the compound prepositional phrase *in order to*.

> <u>Correct</u>
> *To* write more concisely, eliminate compound prepositional phrases.

Notice that by deleting the prepositional phrase, *in order*, the writer eliminated an unnecessary preposition and wordy baggage.

Incorrect
At this point in time, we are writing well.

This sentence contains the compound prepositional phrase *at this point in time.*

Correct
Now, we are writing well.

The writer eliminated the wordy compound prepositional phrase *at this point in time* and replaced it with the simple preposition *now.*

Incorrect
I am writing *with reference to* the new city park.

This sentence is written incorrectly because the writer has used the compound prepositional phrase *with reference to.*

Correct
I am writing *about* the new city park.

Here, the writer replaced the compound prepositional phrase *with reference to* with the simple preposition *about.*

Below are some examples of compound prepositional phrases along with simple prepositions that you should use instead.

Compound Prepositional Phrase	Simple Preposition
at this point in time	now
at that point in time	then
by means of	by
by reason of	because
during the course of	during
for the purpose of	for
in excess of	more
in relation to	concerning, about
in terms of	in

in close proximity to	near
with reference to	about, concerning
with regard to	about, concerning
in a manner similar to	like
on the basis of	by, from
in the event that	if
in order to	to
in favor of	for
for the reason that	because
by virtue of	by
in accordance with	in
in connection with	with

Use the following exercise to help you learn how to eliminate ***compound prepositional phrases*** from your writing.

BRAIN TICKLERS!
Set #4
THE DANGERS OF SMOKING

For each of the sentences below, underline the ***compound prepositional phrase***. Replace the compound prepositional phrase with a ***simple preposition*** or a ***compound preposition***. Write your new sentence on the line provided below the original sentence.

EXAMPLE:

At this point in time, it is clear that smoking is extremely bad for your health.

Now, it is clear that smoking is extremely bad for your health.

1. There are many important facts with reference to smoking.

2. Each year, 390,000 Americans die on the basis of the effects of smoking.

3. With reference to the risk of heart attacks, smokers have more than twice the risk.

4. On the basis of research, it is known that even smoking as few as one to four cigarettes a day can have serious health consequences.

5. Cigarette smoking is addictive for the reason that the nicotine in cigarette smoke causes an addiction.

6. The tobacco industry advertises in order to convince people that smoking is safe and glamorous.

7. Most people begin smoking as teens by reason of their friends are smoking.

8. In order to increase your chances of not smoking, avoid people who do.

9. Smoking causes in excess of 80 percent of all lung cancers.

10. On the basis of all the scientific knowledge available, starting to smoke is one of the worst decisions that you can make.

(Answers are on page 257.)

After working through this chapter, you should be familiar with prepositions and prepositional phrases. Now, it's time to look at another important part of speech—***conjunctions.***

CHAPTER SIX

Conjunctions

In the previous chapter, you learned how prepositions act to "glue" some nouns to the rest of the sentence. This chapter talks about another part of speech that glues or joins words together. These joining words are known as ***conjunctions***. Conjunctions make it possible for you to write about more than one thing in a sentence.

WHAT ARE CONJUNCTIONS?

A ***conjunction*** is a word that joins words or groups of words in a sentence. The most common conjunctions are **and**, **or**, and **but**, and they are also some of the most commonly used words in the English language. Consequently, it's not too difficult to write a few sentences using these familiar words.

> My friends *and* I are going to the mall.
> We are going today *or* tomorrow.
> I want to go to the mall today, *but* my friends want to go to the mall tomorrow.

As with the other parts of speech, you can group them to make conjunctions easier to learn. You can divide conjunctions into three main groups. Let's start with the group containing the most commonly used conjunctions—***coordinating conjunctions***.

COORDINATING CONJUNCTIONS

A ***coordinating conjunction*** connects words or word groups that perform the same function in a sentence. As you will see, that means they **connect** nouns to nouns, verbs to verbs, phrases to phrases, and clauses to clauses. The seven coordinating conjunctions are listed below:

- *but* (joins two contrasting ideas)
- *or* (offers a choice between two or more people, things, or ideas)
- *yet* (means "but")

- *for* (means "because")
- *and* (means "in addition to")
- *nor* (joins two negative alternatives)
- *so* (shows the second idea is the result of the first)

Except for *for* and *so*, coordinating conjunctions can either connect words to words, phrases to phrases, independent clauses to independent clauses, or subordinate clauses to subordinate clauses.

The examples below illustrate how coordinating conjunctions join a **word to a word**. Coordinating conjunctions most often connecting a word to a word are *and* and *or*.

Carlos *and* Marta are coming to my birthday party.

In the above sentence, the coordinating conjunction *and* joins the compound subject, which is two proper nouns, **Carlos** and **Marta**. The coordinating conjunction *and* means "in addition to." Think of it as a plus sign (+).

We can hike *or* swim after we eat our picnic lunch.

Here, the coordinating conjunction *or* connects the compound predicate, which consists of two verbs **hike** and **swim**. The coordinating conjunction *or* tells you that a choice can be made between two activities.

Isis never drinks soft drinks *nor* juice.

In the above sentence, the coordinating conjunction *nor* connects the two nouns **soft drinks** and **juice** by offering each as a choice not taken. *Nor* is the negative form of *or*. It should be used only in negative sentences, which means it must follow grammatically negative words such as **no**, **not**, **never,** and **neither**.

Coordinating conjunctions can also connect phrases. Remember, a **phrase** is group of words without a subject or predicate. In Chapter Five, for example, you learned about prepositional phrases, such as *on the table* and *over the hill.* Below are examples showing coordinating conjunctions joining a **phrase to a phrase**.

Out of sight *and* **out of mind** is a familiar expression.

In the above sentence, the coordinating conjunction *and* joins the phrase **out of sight** to the phrase **out of mind**.

> Abraham Lincoln was a man **of few words** *but* **of many deeds**.

In this example, the coordinating conjunction *but* joins the phrase **of few words** to the phrase **of many deeds** by showing their contrast.

Finally, coordinating conjunctions can connect **clauses**. You will recall that a clause differs from a phrase in that a clause contains a subject and a predicate. There are two types of clauses: *subordinate clauses* and *independent clauses*. A **subordinate clause** has a subject and a predicate but does not express a complete thought. By contrast, an **independent clause** express a complete thought, so it is a sentence.

Let's first see how coordinating conjunctions join subordinate clauses.

> Pham could not remember where **he left his books** or when **he handed in his homework**.

In this example, the coordinating conjunction *or* joins the subordinate clause **he left his books** to the subordinate clause **he handed in his homework**.

Now, let's see how a coordinating conjunction can join two independent clauses. Coordinating conjunctions usually occur in the middle of the sentence, and usually following a comma.

> **Juan worries about his grades**, *yet* **he always does well**.

Here, the coordinating conjunction *yet* joins the independent clause **Juan worries about his grades** to the independent clause **he always does well**. Notice how the coordinating conjunction *yet* can be used in place of the coordinating conjunction *but*.

The coordinating conjunctions *for* and *so* only connect independent clauses, but not words and phrases. Notice the following example.

> **It was raining**, *so* **the bus was late**.

In this example, the coordinating conjunction *so* joins the independent clause **It was raining** to the independent clause

the bus was late by showing that the second clause is the result of the first clause.

Try the following exercise to practice using ***coordinating conjunctions.***

BRAIN TICKLERS!
Set #1
EARTHQUAKES

Use ***coordinating conjunctions*** (**but**, **or**, **yet**, **for**, **and**, **nor**, **so**) to join the two sentences in each problem. Write the new sentence on the line provided.

EXAMPLE:

We know that earthquakes have occurred since the time the planet Earth was formed. We are confident that they will continue to occur in the future.

We know that earthquakes have occurred since the time the planet Earth was formed, **and** we are confident that they will continue to occur in the future.

1. We know earthquakes occur. What causes them?

____

2. This shaking of the ground beneath our feet is usually not harmful. This shaking sometimes causes much property damage and deaths.

____

3. Scientists have studied what causes the rocks to release their energy. They feel if they understand this, they might be able to predict where and when an earthquake will occur.

____

4. The shaking of the ground is caused by an abrupt shifting of rock along fracture lines within the planet Earth. We refer to these fracture lines as *faults*.

5. Scientists know that the rocks release their trapped energy when large sections of the Earth's rocky outer shell shift along a fault and break. No one can accurately predict when this shifting will occur next.

6. A hard outer crust covers the planet Earth. This outer crust is not solid, rather it is broken into massive rock pieces called *tectonic plates*.

7. The ground beneath our feet seems rock-solid. A grid of slowly moving *tectonic plates* of rock composes our planet's surface.

8. Most of the movement occurs along narrow zones between plates. This is where the earthquakes occur.

9. The tectonic plates release great energy when they move. They move only at about the speed that your fingernails grow.

10. Sudden movement of the plates can release the energy trapped in the rock layers. It can be released by a volcanic eruption. Manmade explosions can even release it.

(Some possible answers are on page 258.)

Surf's up...

Surf into this site to learn more about *coordinating conjunctions*:

http://www.chompchomp.com/terms/coordinatingconjunctions.htm

You should be familiar with coordinating conjunctions. Now let's look at another group of conjunctions—***correlative conjunctions.***

CORRELATIVE CONJUNCTIONS

Another major group of conjunctions is the ***correlative conjunction***. Like coordinating conjunctions, correlative conjunctions **connect** words or word groups. In contrast, they appear in pairs and are more forceful than coordinating conjunctions. Below are listed the most commonly used pairs of correlative conjunctions:

either . . . or
neither . . . nor
not . . . but
not only . . . but (also)
both . . . and
although . . . yet
whether . . . or

The examples below illustrate how correlative conjunctions are used.

> *Either* you want to go to the movies with me, *or* you don't want to go to the movies with me.

In this sentence, the correlative conjunctions *either* and *or* connect the two clauses: **you want to go to the movies with me** and **you don't want to go to the movies with me**. These clauses are grammatically equivalent to each other.

> *Neither* Ms. Garcia *nor* Mr. Alvarez knew where Pham was.

Here, the correlative conjunction pair *neither* and *nor* connect two proper nouns **Ms. Garcia** and **Mr. Alvarez**.

> We saw *not* one *but* two lions at the zoo.

In this example the correlative conjunction pair *not* and *but* connect the words **one (lion)** and **two lions**.

> Her movements were *not only* unusual *but also* funny.

In the above sentence, the writer connected the words **unusual** and **funny** with the correlative conjunction pair *not only* and *but also*.

The math test was *both* difficult *and* long.

Here, the correlative conjunction pair *both* and *and* connect the adjectives **difficult** and **long**.

Surf's up...

Glide into this site to learn more about *correlative conjunctions*:

http://grammar.uoregon.edu/conjunctions//correlative.html

The following exercise will provide you with a chance to identify ***correlative conjunctions***.

BRAIN TICKLERS!
Set #2
THE IMPORTANCE OF WATER

For each of the sentences below, underline the ***correlative conjunction*** pair.

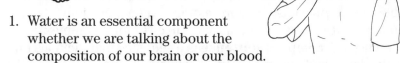

EXAMPLE:

Not only is water everywhere, **but also** it is essential to our survival.

1. Water is an essential component whether we are talking about the composition of our brain or our blood.
2. Not only is the human brain made up of 95 percent water, but also our blood is 80 percent water.
3. Although our body contains a lot of water, yet a 2 percent drop in our body's water supply can lead to *dehydration*.

4. Dehydration, which is a lack of water, has not one but several symptoms.
5. The symptoms range from either being forgetful or having trouble seeing.
6. Although dehydration is one of the most common causes of fatigue, yet many people ignore making sure they drink an adequate amount of water each day.
7. Many people neither are aware they are not drinking enough water nor respond to their thirst by drinking water.
8. As a result, they are either tired or irritable, and sometimes both.
9. Whether serving as a lubricant for our joints or regulating our body temperature through perspiration, water performs important functions.
10. Not only does water help maintain our bodies on a daily basis, but also it helps prevent disease.

(Answers are on page 259.)

Now that you are familiar with correlative conjunctions, let's move on to the last group of conjunctions—***subordinating conjunctions***.

SUBORDINATING CONJUNCTIONS

The final type of conjunction group introduces **subordinate clauses**, and so, we call this group of conjunctions ***subordinating conjunctions***. As you know, not all sentences are composed of grammatically equal parts. Sentences contain **main clauses**, which are clauses that are essential to the main idea. In addition, many sentences also contain **subordinate clauses**, which are clauses that provide additional information about the main clause. Subordinating conjunctions join **subordinate clauses** and **main clauses** to form complex sentences. A **complex sentence** is a sentence that includes one main clause and one or more subordinate clauses. Below is a list of the most common subordinating conjunctions grouped according to the way they connect clauses. The subordinate clauses are single underlined, and the main clauses are double underlined.

Time

after	once	when
as	till	whenever
before	until	while

After social studies class, it is time for lunch.
Before you leave the classroom, hand in your essays.
Until it stops raining, we will have to stay inside.
Whenever I see a snake, I get scared.
When the bell rang, we packed our backpacks.

Stating a Condition

as if	if	unless
as though	provided (that)	how
where	wherever	

Juan hangs around my house *as if* he lives here.
He acts *as though* I should have known he wanted to go with me.
If you want a good grade on the test, you have to study.
I will go to the store *provided that* you go with me.
Unless you can find someone to give you a ride, you will have to take the bus.
My new puppy wants to go *wherever* I go.
We walked past *where* the lightning had struck the tree.

Compare and Contrast

although	than	that	though

Although this is Saturday, Mr. Vu is in his classroom.
My brother is taller *than* my father.

I learned in social studies class *that* the Cherokees had their own written language.
I enjoy eating at restaurants *though* I like my mother's cooking.

Cause and Effect

because   since

I did well on the test *because* I had studied.
Since it was raining, we decided to stay inside.

Surf's up...

Do you want to learn more about *subordinating conjunctions*? If you do, look at this site:

http://www2.gsu.edu/~wwwesl/egw/bryson.hom#list%20sub

BRAIN TICKLERS!
Set #3
FIRE SAFETY

For each of the sentences below, underline the ***subordinating conjunction***.

EXAMPLE:

Although we have seen fires on television, most people don't know much about fires.

1. Before you know it, a small flame can turn into a major house fire.

2. Once a fire gets started, it takes only minutes for it to fill a house with smoke.
3. Because most fires occur when people are sleeping, they can burn for a while before anyone in the house notices.
4. If you wake up to fire, the dark smoke will disorient you.
5. Unless you have prepared beforehand, you may not do the things you need to do to help yourself and your family.

6. Although you think you will know what to do, you and your family should plan and practice what each person will do in case of a fire.
7. Although we usually think about the flames, the heat and smoke from the fire are more dangerous.
8. Once the fire gets burning, temperatures can reach 500 degrees or more at your eye level.
9. If you inhale air that hot, it will scorch your lungs.
10. Because the air is not as hot at floor level, you should stay low as you make your way out of your house.

(Answers are on page 259.)

You have learned about the different groups of conjunctions and how they help you connect words, and now you are ready to learn about the last part of speech—***interjections***.

CHAPTER SEVEN

Interjections

Wow! This is the last chapter about parts of speech. In this chapter, you are going to learn about words such as *wow*. *Wow* and other words of exclamation are called ***interjections***. Use them to show surprise, excitement, anger, happiness, or other strong emotion.

WHAT ARE INTERJECTIONS?

An ***interjection*** is a word or group of words that expresses a feeling or an emotion such as anger, surprise, pain, or happiness. Listed below are some common interjections:

ah	goodness	oh dear	wow	uh oh
oh my	hooray	oh no	hurrah	oh
shh	ouch	okay	aha	ugh

USING INTERJECTIONS

Although the interjection is considered a part of speech, it has no grammatical relationship to the other words around it. Its purpose is to allow the writer to express a feeling or an emotion. Use an *exclamation point* (!) after an interjection that expresses **strong** feeling or emotion. By contrast, use a *comma* (,) after an interjection that expresses **mild** feeling or emotion. Below are some examples of interjections and how they are used in written English.

Aha! I thought you were the one who planned my surprise birthday party!
Hooray! Our soccer team is in first place!
"Wow!" I can't believe it's Friday already!
Ouch! I hit my finger with the hammer!
Oh, I'm sorry. I didn't see you standing there.
"Shh," whispered Ms. Garcia. "You have to be quiet while the others are finishing their tests."

Surf's up...

Surf on into this site to learn more about *interjections*:

http://www.englishclub.com/vocabulary/interjections.htm

Use the following exercise to help you to identify ***interjections*** and see how they are used.

BRAIN TICKLERS!
Set #1
THE ANCIENT OLYMPICS

For each of the exercises below, underline the ***interjection***.

EXAMPLE:

Wow! Did you know the first Olympics were held over 2700 years ago in 776 B.C.?

1. "Aha!" exclaimed Pham. I learned the Olympic games got their name from Olympia, the Greek city where they first took place.
2. Ah, like the Olympics of today, the ancient Olympics were held every four years.
3. Oh my, this is interesting. All wars were stopped during the Olympics so that the athletes and spectators could enjoy the competition.
4. Goodness! There was only one event in the first Olympics!

5. Wow! What was the event?
6. Okay, it was a foot race—a 200-meter race.
7. Ah, but over time they added other events to the games.
8. Hooray! I like to watch all of them!
9. Oh, and the ancient Olympics were religious—they were held to honor Zeus, the leader of the gods.
10. Hooray! I'm happy we can enjoy the Olympics!

(Answers are on page 260.)

Wow! Congratulations! You have finished the last section on parts of speech. As you have learned, parts of speech are important tools of the English language. Now, it's time to learn about another important tool—***spelling and vocabulary***.

CHAPTER EIGHT

Spelling and Vocabulary

In this chapter you will learn about ***spelling*** and ***vocabulary***. Spelling words properly is important because misspelled words will distract the reader from what you are trying to say. When you write words that sound or look like the words you are intending to use but have different meaning, you will confuse your reader.

For instance, if you write: The *fair* for my *plain* ticket was about $200.00.
When you should have written: The **fare** for my **plane** ticket was about $200.00.

Your reader has to stop and think about what you meant!

This chapter will help you become a good speller, and it will give you the opportunity to review and learn a lot of vocabulary words. Yet having an extensive vocabulary is up to you. Not only will you have to follow the lessons of this chapter, but you will also have to read a lot of books to become familiar with new words and increase your vocabulary.

ACTIVE LISTENING

The key to becoming a good speller and having a large vocabulary is active listening. ***Active listening*** is focusing your attention on the speaker or teacher to understand what he or she is saying. How do you actively listen? First, you look at the speaker and concentrate. Avoid any distractions around you. Then, follow and understand what the speaker is saying. Active listening does not mean that you have to agree with what the speaker says or that what the speaker is saying is interesting! It means that you understand what is being said, and you respond to questions and directions. An important part of active listening is not interrupting the speaker! Active listening is hard to do, but it pays off by helping you remember what the speaker said or, when it comes to spelling, how to pronounce words correctly.

You must actively listen for the correct pronunciation of the word and then use a dictionary to find the correct spelling. Remember that a dictionary can also give you the correct pronunciation of a word using a pronunciation key. To help you with pronunciation of some words that you are not familiar with, the pronunciation key for the *American Heritage College Dictionary* has been inserted in this book's appendix.

Surf's up...

To learn more about *active listening*, check out this site:

http://www.eslteachersboard.com/cgi-bin/lessons/index.pl?noframes;read=912

When you are actively listening, you will hear words much more clearly. Hearing the words clearly will help you to pronounce them yourself and become familiar with certain sounds. Learning these sounds will help you become a better speller. Let's look at these sounds.

LEARNING THE VOWEL SOUNDS

Short and Long Vowel Sounds

The letters **a, e, i, o, u** represent one or more vowel sounds. It is important to know that a vowel is not a letter but rather the sound representation of that letter. Short vowel sounds are usually spelled by the single vowel they represent followed by a consonant sound. They are called **short vowels sounds** because we pronounce them for a shorter time than the **long vowel sounds**. In addition, long vowel sounds are not always spelled with the letter whose name you hear.

IMPORTANT!

Phonetic sounds are shown in brackets /ă/.

For correct pronunciations, use an online dictionary such as Merriam-Webster Online dictionary at http://www.m-w.com/dictionary/

Short Vowel Sound a / ă / with Long Vowel Sound a /ā/

Words with the **short vowel sound /ă/** have the following spelling pattern:

Words with **–a** like *act, cat, man, and plant*

Examples of other words with the sound /ă/ that do not conform to the above spelling pattern are Fr**ance**, l**ance**, d**ance**, c**al**f, h**al**f, and l**au**gh.

Words with the **long vowel sound /ā/** have six common spelling patterns:

Words with **–a** like *favor, flavor, savor*
Words with **–a_e** like *bake, cake, tame* (silent *e*)
Words with **–a_ _e** like *ache, baste, paste*
Words with **-ai** like *drain, gain, pain*
Words with **–ai_e** like *braise, maize, praise* (silent *e*)
Words with **-ay** like *gray, pray, say*

There are many words with the sound **/ā/** that do not conform to the categories above like cr**e**pe, gr**ea**t, matin**ee**, v**ei**l, n**eigh**bor, bouqu**et**, and pr**ey**.

Before you go on to the e vowel sounds, try the following exercises to make sure that you understand short vowel sound a /ă/ with long vowel sound a /ā/.

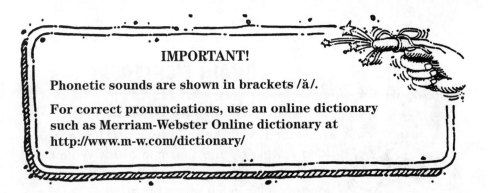

BRAIN TICKLERS!

Set #1

CLIMATE AND WEATHER

The sounds with the short vowel **/ă/** and the long vowel **/ā/** are shown in **bold**. Write the word plus SVă for short vowel ă or LVā for long vowel ā in the space provided.

EXAMPLE:

My father's bl**a**ck cow h**a**d one c**a**lf yesterd**ay**.

bl**a**ck SVă   h**a**d SVă   c**a**lf SVā   yesterd**ay** LVā

1. Climate ch**a**nge refers to ch**a**nges in our climate that h**a**ve occurred since the early part of the 1900s.

   ____

2. Weather is the st**a**te of the **a**tmosphere **at a** given time and pl**a**ce.

   ____

3. **A**tmospheric g**a**ses are mostly nitrogen (78 percent) and oxygen (21 percent).

   ____

4. **A**cid r**ai**n is formed when sulfur dioxide combines with water v**a**por in the **a**tmosphere.

   ____

5. **A** m**a**jor volc**a**nic eruption m**ay** cause a prolonged decrease in the temperature of Earth's **a**tmosphere.

   ____

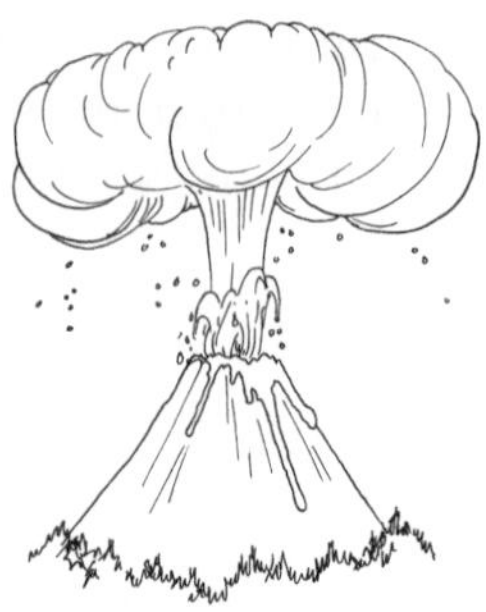

6. Ev**a**por**a**tion, runoff, and precipit**a**tion are part of the global water b**a**lance.

   ____

7. Thunder is the sound produced by exp**a**nding g**a**ses along the p**a**th of **a** lightning fl**a**sh.

____

8. H**ai**l is formed in thunderhead clouds **a**nd falls along p**a**ths scientists call *hail swaths*.

____

9. Hurric**a**nes g**a**ther heat and energy through cont**a**ct with warm ocean waters.

____

10. Ozone, **a** colorless g**a**s, is harmful to humans, but beneficial in the str**a**tosphere by absorbing most of the sun's ultraviolet radi**a**tion.

____

(Answers are on page 260.)

Short Vowel Sound e /ĕ/ with Long Vowel Sound e /ē/

Let's now go over short vowel sound e /ĕ/ with long vowel sound e /ē/. Words with the **short vowel sound e /ĕ/** have the following spelling patterns:

> Words with **–e** like *get, met, pet, set*
> Words with **–ea** like *bread, dread, tread*

Examples of other words with less usual spelling patterns but that use the short vowel sound /ĕ/ are **a**ny, s**ai**d, l**ei**sure, l**eo**pard, b**ury,** and g**ue**ss.

Words with the **long vowel sound e /ē/** have the following spelling patterns:

> Words with **–e** like *be, he, me*
> Words with **–e_e** like *genes, scene*
> Words with **–ea** like *meal, peal, seal*
> Words with **–ee** like *peek, meek, seek*
> Word with **–y** like *daffy, happy, pappy*

There are many words with the long vowel sound e /ē/ that do not conform to the categories above like p**ea**ce, rec**ei**ve, th**ie**f, k**ey**, curi**o**us, and mach**ine**.

Before you go on to the next vowel, work through the following exercises.

BRAIN TICKLERS!
Set #2
CALIFORNIA EXPLORERS AND SETTLERS

The sounds with the short vowel **/ĕ/** and the long vowel **/ē/** are shown in **bold**. Write the word plus SVĕ for short vowel ĕ or LVē for long vowel ē in the space provided.

EXAMPLE:

I dr**e**ad to **e**at my aunt's br**e**ad.

dread SVĕ eat LVē bread = SVĕ

1. **Sea e**xploration by Europ**ea**ns was possible due to many t**e**chnological dev**e**lopments like the s**e**xtant and the chronometer.

2. Francisco Vásqu**e**z de Coronado l**e**d one of the most remarkable Europ**ea**n **e**xplorations of the North Am**e**rican Southw**e**st.

3. In 1536, Cort**e**z l**e**d an **e**xpedition that **e**xplored the Pacific coast of M**e**xico and discovered Baja California.

4. In 1542, a thr**ee**-vessel armada under the command of Juan Rodrígu**e**z Cabrillo, l**e**ft Navidad on the w**e**st coast of M**e**xico.

5. The expedition sailed north and explored the Baja Peninsula until the fleet made landfall at San Diego Bay in September.

____

6. Sebastian Vizcaíno was one of the first European explorers to reach Monterey in December 1602.

____

7. They went ashore the next day and pitched the church tent under the shade of an oak tree.

____

8. The Portolá expedition set out from San Diego on July 14, 1769 and reached Los Angeles on August 2.

____

9. Spain and later Mexico gave people land grants to start ranchos and encourage settlers.

____

10. Because of the Gold Rush, some settlers left the East Coast and traveled to Panama. There, they crossed the isthmus and took a ship heading north to California.

____

(Answers are on page 260.)

Short Vowel Sound i /ĭ/ with Long Vowel Sound i /ī/

Now you are ready to learn about short vowel sound /ĭ/ with long vowel sound /ī/. Words with the short **vowel sound i /ĭ/** have the following spelling patterns:

Words with **–e** like *English*
Words with **–i** like *bit, pit, lit*

Examples of other words with less usual spelling patterns, but using the short vowel sound i /ĭ/ are advant**age**, carr**ia**ge, b**u**sy, ab**y**ss, w**o**men, and b**ui**ld.

Words with the **long vowel sound i /ī/** have the following spelling patterns:

Words with **–i** like *mild, wild*
Words with **–i_e** like *mile, vile, tile*
Words with **–ie** like *lie, pie, tie*

Words with **–igh** like *sight, might, light*
Words with **–y** like *dye, by, my*

Examples of other words with less usual spelling patterns but that use the long vowel sound i /ī/ are Th**ai**land, pap**aya**, st**ei**n, h**eigh**t, **eye**, **is**land, b**ye**, and rh**yme**.

Before you go on to the next vowel, the following exercises will help you review what you have just learned.

BRAIN TICKLERS!

Set #3

PHYSICAL PROPERTIES OF MATTER

The sounds with the short vowel /ĭ/ and the long vowel /ī/ are shown in **bold**. Write the word plus SVĭ for short vowel ĭ or LVī for long vowel ī in the space provided.

EXAMPLE:

The dr**i**ll**i**ng b**i**t has **i**ndustrial d**i**amonds.

drilling SVĭ   bit SVĭ   industrial SVĭ   diamonds LVī

1. The three states of matter are l**i**qu**i**d, sol**i**d, and gas.

   ____

2. A ph**y**s**i**cal property **i**s anyth**i**ng you can observe about an object us**i**ng your senses.

   ____

3. Matter is everyth**i**ng made of atoms and molecules and anyth**i**ng that has a mass.

   ____

4. Ox**y**gen as a gas st**i**ll has the same properties as l**i**qu**i**d oxygen. Wh**y**? Because oxygen **i**s an element.

   ____

5. The freezing point of a pure liquid is essentially the same as the melting point of the same substance in its solid form.

____

6. When an ice cube melts, a physical change occurs.

____

7. When iron rusts, you can see a chemical change occurring over a long period of time.

____

8. A solid holds its shape, even when you grind it into a powder. Put some of the powder under a microscope and you will see the same shape.

____

9. A diamond is a perfect crystal lattice, which is a very exact organization of atoms.

____

10. Liquids are an in-between state of matter positioned between the solid and gas states.

____

(Answers are on page 261.)

Short Vowel Sound o /ŏ/ with Long Vowel Sound o /ō/

Words with the **short vowel sound o /ŏ/** have the following spelling patterns:

Words with **-o** like *block, odd, shock*

Examples of other words with less usual spelling patterns but that use the short vowel sound /ŏ/ are c**o**ugh, J**o**hn, astron**au**t, w**a**sh, and tr**au**ma. Words with the **long vowel sound o /ō/** have the following spelling patterns:

Words with **-o** like *no, so, torso*
Words with **-o_e** like *mole, pole, sole*
Words with **-oa** like *boat, coat, moat*
Words with **-oe** like *doe, foe, toe*
Words with **-ow** like *mow, sow, tow*

There are many words with the long vowel sound o /ō/ that do not conform to the categories above like plat**eau**, **oh**, **folk**, s**ou**l, and th**ough.**

Before you go on to the next vowel, try the following exercises.

BRAIN TICKLERS!

Set #4

THE SOLAR SYSTEM

The sounds with the short vowel /ŏ/ and the long vowel /ō/ are shown in **bold**. Write the word plus SVŏ for short vowel ŏ or LVō for long vowel ō in the space provided.

EXAMPLE:

The human b**o**dy is m**o**stly water.

body SVŏ mostly LVō

1. The s**o**lar system consists of the sun and the **o**bjects that orbit around it.

 ____

2. A planet does n**o**t give off its **ow**n light.

 ____

3. The f**ou**r planets cl**o**sest to the sun are inner planets: Mercury, Venus, Earth, and Mars.

 ____

4. Inner planets have r**o**cky surfaces, they are warmer and smaller than m**o**st of the outer planets, and none of them has more than two moons.

 ____

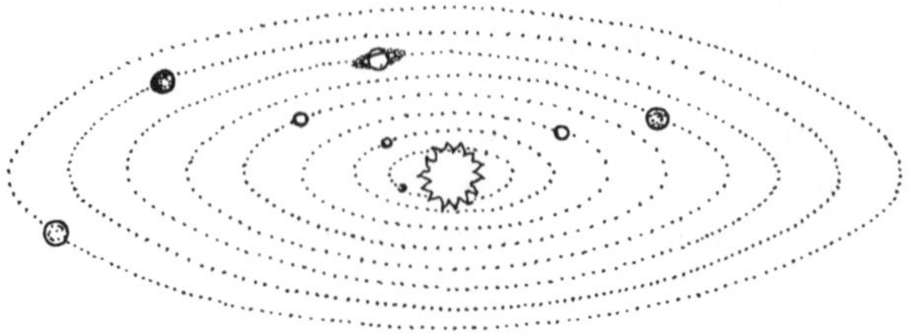

5. Earth is the **o**nly planet kn**ow**n to support life.

____

6. Earth has two movements: r**o**tation and revolution. It r**o**tates **o**n its axis every 24 hours. It completes one revolution around the sun every 365¼ days.

____

7. Gravity is the force that h**o**lds the planets in orbit around the sun.

____

8. Jupiter is the s**o**lar system's largest planet; Plut**o** is a dwarf planet.

____

9. Black sp**o**ts on the surface of the sun are kn**ow**n as sunsp**o**ts.

____

10. The J**o**vian or gas planets are Jupiter, Saturn, Uranus, and Mars. They are comp**o**sed primarily of r**o**ck and metal, they have sl**ow** r**o**tation, and s**o**lid surfaces.

____

(Answers are on page 261.)

Let's now review **short vowel sound /ŭ/ with long vowel sound u /o͞o/ and long u with y in front /yo͞o/**. We are almost done with vowel sounds!

Words with the **short vowel sound u /ŭ/** have the following spelling patterns:

Words with –o like *once, one, oven*
Words with –u like *but, cut, hut*

Other words with less usual spelling patterns but that use the short vowel sound u /ŭ/ are fl**oo**d, tr**ou**ble, d**oe**s.

Words with the **long vowel sound u /o͞o/** have the following spelling patterns:

Words with –ew like *drew, flew, stew*
Words with –o like *to, do*
Words with –oo like *soon, moon, spoon*
Words with –o_e like *lose, whose*
Words with –u like *Luther, Ruth*
Words with –u_e like in *dune, June, tune*

Other words with less usual spelling patterns, but using the long vowel sound u /o͞o/ are can**oe**, y**ou**, S**ue**, s**ui**t, thr**ough**, t**wo.**

Words with the **long vowel sound u with y in front /yo͞o/** have the following spelling patterns:

> Words with –ew like *ewe, pew, pewter*
> Words with –u like *human, humid, humility*
> Words with –u_e like *huge, mule*

Other words with less usual spelling patterns, but using the long vowel sound u with y in front /yo͞o/ are: f**eu**d, vi**ew**, barbec**ue**, be**au**ty

Before you go on to the next vowel, try the following exercises as a review.

BRAIN TICKLERS!

Set #5

Properties of Metals

The sounds with the short vowel /ŭ/, long vowel /o͞o/, and long vowel /yo͞o/ are shown in **bold**. Write the word plus SVŭ for short vowel ŭ, LVo͞o for long vowel o͞o, and LVyo͞o for long vowel yo͞o in the space provided.

EXAMPLE:

"Y**ou** sh**ou**ld c**o**me t**o** sch**oo**l everyday!" said the teacher.

you LVo͞o   should LVo͞o   come SVŭ   to LVo͞o   school LVo͞o

1. Metals, like al**u**minum, constit**u**te most of the periodic table.

____

2. Al**u**minum foil is an example of a good cond**u**ctor.

____

3. A silver sp**oo**n cond**u**cts heat easily, b**u**t a w**oo**den spoon would not.

____

4. Passing c**u**rrent thr**ou**gh a wire that is wrapped around an iron core creates a temporary magnet.

____

5. Most metals are chemically **u**nstable, reacting with oxygen to form oxides. Iron r**u**sts over years, b**u**t potassium b**u**rns in seconds.

____

6. Metals are good cond**u**ctors of heat and electricity. They can be melted or f**u**sed.

____

7. *Fusible* is something capable of being f**u**sed or melted by heating.

____

8. T**u**ngsten f**u**ses, or melts, only at extremely high temperatures (3370°C).

____

9. Al**u**minum (Al), iron (Fe), nickel (Ni), copper (Cu), silver (Ag), and gold (Au) are p**u**re elements.

____

10. St**u**dents, are all metals magnetic? No, silver, gold, copper, and al**u**minum are not.

____

(Answers are on page 262.)

Now, let's go over the **schwa sound /ə/**.

To understand the **schwa** sound you need to understand what a syllable is. A syllable is a **vowel sound**, either by itself or with the preceding and following consonant sounds. It is a sound produced by a single vocal impulse. The following words are separated by their syllables:

tyrant ty•rant   telegraph tel•e•graph   decimal dec•i•mal

In English, when you speak, you stress (emphasize) certain syllables and nonstress others. Stress is the relative emphasis given to certain syllables in a word. Stressed syllables have higher pitch, longer duration, and typically fuller vowels than unstressed syllables. Look at the previous words, the stressed syllable is shown in **bold**.

ty•rant **tel**•e•graph **dec**•i•mal

When the sound of short u appears in an <u>unstressed</u> syllable, you call that the sound *schwa*. Thus, the ***a*** in tyr**a**nt, the second ***e*** in tel**e**graph, and the ***i*** in dec**i**mal are all schwa sounds. Other words with schwa sounds are ***a***, ***for***, ***of***, ***was***, ***the***, and ***about***. The schwa sound is represented by the symbol ə.

BRAIN TICKLERS!

Set #6

THE AMERICAN REVOLUTION

Use the dictionary to find any **schwa** sound in any word except "a" and "of," in the sentences below. When you find them, <u>underline</u> the vowel. Remember: The schwa sound only happens on unstressed syllables.

EXAMPLE:

The scientific method is used to discover the answer to a scientific problem.

The sci<u>e</u>ntific meth<u>o</u>d is used to discov<u>e</u>r the answ<u>e</u>r to a sci<u>e</u>ntific probl<u>e</u>m.

1. Before the Seven Years War, the thought of severing the bond with Britain was inconceivable.
2. There were forces at work for many years that would eventually dissolve the political bond between Britain and the colonists.
3. James Otis, a Boston lawyer, addressed the Superior Court and urged people to resist.
4. It sounded the first note of resistance to British authority heard in the colonies.

5. Patrick Henry said, "a king, from being a father to his people, degenerates into a tyrant, and forfeits all right to obedience."
6. In 1754, the French and Indian War saw the British pitted against the French, the Austrians, and the Spanish.
7. In 1758, William Pitt came out of retirement, and by the end of the year, the British had begun to turn the tide in the war in North America.
8. In 1764, the British imposed, for the first time, a series of taxes designed to raise revenue from the colonies.
9. The Stamp Act of 1765 hurt the colonists' pocketbooks.
10. In the year of 1767, Charles Townshend, Chancellor of the Exchequer, convinced Parliament to pass a series of laws imposing new taxes on the colonists.

(Answers are on page 262.)

LEARNING THE R SOUNDS

The /âr/ sound

Words with the **/âr/ sound** have the following spelling patterns:

Words with **–air** like *lair, fair, hair*
Words with **–ar** like *Mary, parent, rare*
Words with **–are** like in *snare, fare, care*
Words with **–ear** like in *pear, bear, tear*

Other words with less usual spelling patterns using the /âr/ sound are **aer**obic, million**aire**, pr**ayer**, and h**eir.**

The /îr/ sound

Words with the **/îr/ sound** have the following spelling patterns:

Words with **–ear** like in *dear, tear, fear*
Words with **–eer** like in *deer, veneer, peer*
Words with **–er** like Ceres, *cero, zero*
Words with **–ere** like *here, mere*

Other words with less usual spelling using the /îr/ sound are w**eir**d, t**ier**, and th**eory**.

The /ôr/ sound

Words with the **/ôr/ sound** have the following spelling patterns:

Words with **–ar** like *barrel, quarrel, quarry*
Words with **–or** like *condor, Labrador, matador*
Words with **–ore** like *ore, galore, more*

Words with less usual spelling using the /ôr/ sound are cent**aur**, r**oar**, d**oor**, and f**our.**

The /ûr/ sound

Words with the **/ûr/ sound** have the following spelling patterns:

Words with **–ear** like in *hearse, learn, pearl*
Words with -**er** like *kerfs, kern, kernel*
Words with **–ir** like *bird, flirt, sir*
Words with **–or** like word, *work, worm*
Words with **–ur** like *burn, turn urn*

Words with less usual spelling using the /ûr/ sound are w**ere**, entrepren**eur**, wh**irr**, c**our**tesy, and b**urr.**

The final /∂r/ sound

Words with the **final /∂r/** sound have the following spelling patterns:

Words with **–ar** like *burglar, lunar, pillar*
Words with **–er** like *thunder, powder, matter*
Words with **–or** like *actor, flavor, tractor*

BRAIN TICKLERS!

Set #7

MORE ABOUT THE AMERICAN REVOLUTION

In each sentence write the words with the **R sounds** and specify which sound it is by writing /âr/, /îr/, /ôr/, /ûr/, or /∂r/.

1. Where did British troops land in 1767 to restore order? They landed in Boston.

____

2. The Boston Massacre took place in 1770. Later that year, the colonists learned that the Townshend Act had been repealed except for tea.

____

3. On June 9, 1772, the British revenue schooner, the *Gaspee*, ran aground south of Providence, Rhode Island, and that night it was burned.

____

4. On December 16, 1773, farmers and Bostonians met to hear their speaker Samuel Adams. Later that evening the Boston Tea Party incident took place.

____

5. The Coercive Acts of 1774 included the closing of the port of Boston, until the East India Tea Company received compensation for the tea dumped in the harbor.

____

6. King George III misdirected policies toward the colonists contributed to the American Revolution.

____

7. The colonists were united in their belief that Britain had no right to tax them.

____

8. The First Continental Congress met in 1774 in Philadelphia's Carpenters Hall.

____

9. There, twelve of the thirteen colonies were present.

____

10. The American Revolution chief result was the birth of the first federal government in history.

____

(Answers are on page 262.)

THE SILENT LETTERS

Edward Carney, author of *A Survey of English Spelling*, distinguishes two kinds of silent letters: *auxiliary* and *dummy*.

Auxiliary letters are part of a group of letters that spell a sound that does not have a usual single letter to represent it. For example,

/th/ thing **/th/** there **/sh/** share **/zh/** treasure **/ng/** song

Dummy letters have two subgroups: **inert letters** and **empty letters. Inert letters** are letters that in a given word segment are sometimes heard and sometimes not heard. For example,

resign (g is not heard) **resignation** (g is heard)
malign (g is not heard) **malignant** (g is heard)

Empty letters are letters that do not have a function like auxiliary letters or inert letters. The letter *u* in the word gauge is empty. Here are some examples of silent consonants:

Silent b: dumb, thumb
Silent c: indict
Silent ch: yacht
Silent d: bridge, ledge, edge
Silent g: foreign, sign, design, assign
Silent h: rhinoceros, spaghetti
Silent k: knee, knit, knob, know, knuckle
Silent l: calf, talk, could, should, would
Silent m: mnemonic
Silent n: autumn, column
Silent p: raspberry, receipt
Silent t: castle, listen, whistle
Silent w: answer, wrap, wreath, wreck, wring, wrong, write

There are no rules that we can apply to words with empty letters, you just have to use them and remember their spelling.

THE FINAL E

Markers are letters that do not represent a sound, they are silent, but they tell you something about the sound of other letters in the word. **Silent e** is an example of a marker. It signals a long vowel sound in the syllable it finishes. Look at the following pair of words:

mat	mate
fat	fate
hat	hate

Notice that the short a in mat, fat, and hat are converted to a long a when silent e finishes the words. They become mate, fate, and hate.

BRAIN TICKLERS!
Set #8
SPELLING CORRECTLY

Circle the correct spelling for the words in brackets in each sentence.

1. (Lisen, Listen) to the sounds of birds. Birds lack vocal cords and produce sounds through vibrations sent across their *syrinx* or voice box.
2. A Chef's (knife, neif) is used for most types of chopping, dicing, mincing, and slicing.
3. A (caf, calf) is the young of an animal, and the word is mainly used for cattle.
4. Thomas Jefferson's handwritten draft of the Declaration of Independence is considered a national (treshur, treasure).
5. Read all the (answers, ansers) to each problem before you make your selection.
6. The (mnemonics, nemonics) to remember the planets is "My Very Easy Method Just Simply Uses Nine Planets."

7. The (nee, knee) is the largest joint in the body.
8. Rock, Paper, (Sissors, Scissors) is an extremely popular hand game that is most often played by children.
9. It is (rong, wrong) to pick the first answer you see in a test without examining all the other answers.
10. Astrophysicists (write, rite) about the physical properties of the universe.

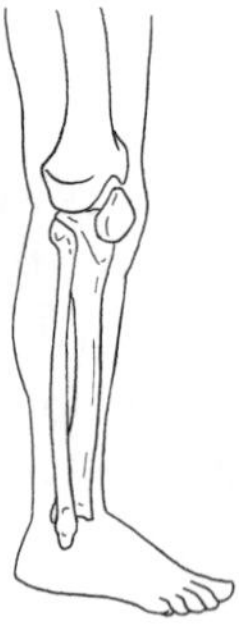

(Answers are on page 263.)

HOMOPHONES

Homophones are words that **sound alike** but have different meanings and spelling. To become proficient in using homophones, you must know the meaning of the word, and you must use them correctly. For example, you would not see this written unless her son was an animal with antlers!

> "Good morning, deer," said the mother to her son.

Instead, you would see this:

> "Good morning, dear," said the mother to her son.

The writer would know to use *dear* instead of *deer*. Why? Because he or she knows that a *deer* refers to a hoofed animal, whereas a *dear* refers to a person.

Let's look at some homophones and a way to tell them apart.

Brake and Break

Brake—a device for slowing or stopping motion.

> My dad's new car has disk **brakes.**

Break—to separate into pieces suddenly or violently.

> I was about to **break** my brother's piggy bank when he entered the room.

Fare and Fair

Fare—a transportation charge (It has other meanings also.)

My **fare** from Houston to New York was $300.00 round-trip.

Fair—light in color (It has other meanings also.)

My roommate has a **fair** complexion and needs to use lots of sunscreen.

Hear and Here

Hear—to perceive sound by the ear

I can **hear** my neighbor's dog barking.

Here—at or in this place

"Goodbye, my bus stop is **here**."

Its and It's

Its—the possessive form of it

The cat ate **its** food in a hurry.

It's—the contraction of it is

My cat is finicky, and **it's** also moody.

To and Too

To—in a direction toward so as to reach

The circus is going **to** the city.

Too—in addition, also

I am going to bed, and you will **too**!

There, Their, and They're

There—at or in that place

There, among the boys, is my little baby girl.

Their—the possessive form of they

Their daughter goes to NYU.

They're—the contraction of they are

> **They're** from Guangzhou, China, and are here studying chemistry.

Surf's up...

If you want to learn more about *homophones*, check out this site:

http://collections.ic.gc.ca/literacy/le/literacy4.htm

PARTS OF A WORD

If you know the structure of words, your vocabulary will increase. The main part of a word is called the *root.* The *root* is the part of the word that contains the basic meaning. A *prefix* is a word element placed before the *root* to modify or change the root's meaning. A *suffix* is a word element placed after the *root* to modify or change the root's meaning.

Here are some common prefixes:

bi (two) biannual, bicycle, bilateral
de (not) deactivate, debunk, decentralize
dis (not) disability, disadvantage, disappear
im (not) immaterial, immeasurable, impossible
mis (not) misalignment, misallocation, misapplication
pre (before) preadmission, preview, preannounce
re (again) reabsorb, reacquire, reactivate

These are some common suffixes:

-er abolisher, absorber, adopter
-able acceptable, accountable, consumable
-ous advantageous, adventurous, cancerous
-ness aimlessness, adeptness, carefulness

-ful bashful, fearful, joyful
-ly abrasively, absolutely, annually
-ment accomplishment, achievement, adjustment

Surf's up...

If you want to learn more about words that begin or end with these *prefixes* or *suffixes*, check out this site:

http://www.morewords.com/combo/

COMPOUND WORDS

Compound words are words made up of two or more whole words that function as a single unit of meaning. There are three categories of compound words:

closed—the words run together (notebook, makeup, redhead)
open—there is a space between the words (half sister, full moon, post office)
hyphenated—the words are connected by a hyphen (two-year-old, mother-in-law, over-the-counter)

Surf's up...

If you want to see a comprehensive list of *compound words*, please check out this site:

http://www.paulnoll.com/China/Teach/English-compound-1.html

With practice, your spelling and vocabulary will continue to improve. Now, it's time to return to writing, and take what you have learned about words and use them to improve your ***writing***.

PART TWO

Writing

CHAPTER NINE

Sentence Endings and Pauses

SENTENCE ENDINGS

For the sake of simplicity, you can divide punctuation into two groups: punctuation that allows you to end a sentence and punctuation that allows you to create a pause within a sentence. Both sets of punctuation are important, but let's begin with sentence endings. There are three types of punctuation that mark the end of a sentence: **periods**, **question marks**, and **exclamation points**.

Periods

Use a ***period*** (.) to end a complete sentence that is a statement, a command, or a request. We call a sentence that makes a statement a **declarative sentence**. Below are examples of declarative sentences.

Isis enjoys singing and dancing.
Our school is located on the corner of Twenty-third Street and North Avenue.

Below are some examples of sentences that make a request or command.

Please close the window.
Turn in your assignment and then you may leave.

Don't use periods at the end of phrases or dependent clauses. If you do, you create sentence fragments, and sentence fragments are not accepted in formal writing. Remember: a **phrase** is a group of words without a subject or a predicate. A **dependent clause** differs from a phrase in that it has a subject and a predicate, but like a phrase, it does not express a complete thought.

Incorrect
At the end of the street. We stopped running.

By incorrectly inserting a period at the end of the phrase *at the end of the street*, the writer created a sentence fragment followed by a sentence.

Correct
At the end of the street, we stopped running.

This sentence is correctly written because the writer has used a period at the end of the sentence, while using a comma (which you will learn more about later in this chapter) to set off the introductory phrase.

You will learn more about **quotation marks** in a bit, but for now, let's just say there are times when you need to write exactly what someone said. We call this a **direct quotation**. To do so, you must use quotation marks (" ") to mark the beginning of the direct quotation as well as at the end of the direct quotation. For instance, the following are examples of direct quotations. Notice the period at the end of the sentence and its location <u>inside</u> of the quotation marks when the quotation marks are at the end of the sentence.

> Carlos said, "I have finished my homework."
> Pham said, "I still have a few problems left, but I will be finished soon."

Because most sentences are declarative sentences, a period is the most often used punctuation for ending sentences. Nevertheless, you will also need to write other types of sentences, such as ones that ask a **question**.

Question Marks

We refer to sentences that ask a question as **interrogative sentences**. You must write a ***question mark (?)*** at the end of an interrogative sentence. The job of the question mark is to end a question.

> What time is it?
> Do you know the answer?

Interrogative sentences require only one ending punctuation mark, so use only a question mark, not a question mark and a period.

> <u>Incorrect</u>
> Where is the swimming pool?.

This interrogative sentence is incorrectly punctuated because it contains two sentence endings—a question mark and a period.

> <u>Correct</u>
> Where is the swimming pool?

Now, the interrogative sentence is correctly punctuated because it ends with only a question mark.

Question Marks with Quotation Marks

Let's look at the situation where you want to write the exact question that someone asked. To do this, you will need to use quotation marks as well as a question mark. The following examples show you how to write this question correctly. Notice how the question mark is <u>inside</u> the quotation marks.

> Ugo asked, "What time is the bus coming?"
> Pham asked, "What time does the schedule say the bus should arrive?"

IMPORTANT!

When a question is being written about rather than directly asked, this is called an *indirect question*. Sentences containing indirect questions should end with a period, rather than a question mark. Compare the following sentences:

<u>Direct Question</u>

Juan asked, "Which animals did you see at the zoo?"

<u>Indirect Question</u>

Juan asked which animals we saw at the zoo.

Exclamation Points

As you learned in Chapter Seven, ***exclamation points (!)*** follow **interjections.** For instance,

> Wow!
> Hooray!

Exclamation points also end sentences that show excitement or strong emotion. We refer to these sentences as **exclamatory sentences**. It is as if the entire sentence acts as an interjection.

Consequently, all exclamatory sentences must end with an exclamation point.

> Wow! Look at the size of that fish!
> That is the biggest fish that I have ever seen!

As you learned with question marks, use only one punctuation mark to end an exclamatory sentence. This means that you must use only an exclamation point, not an exclamation point and a period.

> <u>Incorrect</u>
> Oh no! We missed the bus!.

This sentence is incorrect because the writer used both an exclamation point and a period at the end of the exclamatory sentence.

> <u>Correct</u>
> Oh no! We missed the bus!

Now the sentence is properly punctuated because the exclamatory sentence ends only with an exclamation point.

Imperative Sentences

Exclamation points should also be used to end sentences that command the reader or listener to do something. Sentences that command are called **imperative sentences**. Below are examples of imperative sentences. Notice that each imperative sentence appears to lack a subject, yet it is still a sentence. It is a sentence because these sentences do not write but instead assume that the word *you* (the person being commanded) is the subject.

> Don't touch that! (Don't **you** touch that!)
> Listen to me! (**You** listen to me!)
> Stop teasing that dog! (**You** stop teasing the dog!)

Notice that an imperative sentence can be as short as one word:

Stop!	(**You** stop!)
Run!	(**You** run!)
Look!	(**You** look!)

Surf's up...

If you want to learn more about *sentence endings*, check out this site:

http://esl.about.com/od/englishgrammar/a/a_punctuation.htm

Use the following exercise to help you make sure that you understand how to the use the ***sentence endings*** you have just read about.

BRAIN TICKLERS!
Set #1
DENTAL HEALTH

You have learned about ***sentence endings***: the **period (.)**, the **question mark (?)**, and the **exclamation point (!)**. Write the correct sentence ending at the end of each sentence. Next, on the line provided at the end of each sentence, write whether the sentence is a **declarative**, **interrogative**, **exclamatory**, or **imperative** sentence.

EXAMPLE:

Did you know that everyone has living organisms called *bacteria* living on their teeth, gums, and tongue

Did you know that everyone has living organisms called *bacteria* living on their teeth, gums, and tongue**? interrogative**

1. That's disgusting __________

2. Actually, most of the bacteria are necessary for our health, but some of the bacteria cause problems for humans __________
3. Certain bacteria cause tooth decay __________
4. How do they do that __________
5. These bacteria attach themselves to the hard surface of our teeth, which we refer to as *enamel* __________
6. The bacteria multiply and grow into a *colony* right there on the enamel of our teeth __________

7. Proteins in our saliva mix with the bacteria and form a whitish film called *plaque* on our teeth __________
8. Plaque is harmful because it produces acid that is responsible for destroying the protective enamel of our teeth __________
9. Does that mean a *cavity* is a hole in my tooth __________
10 Brush your teeth after every meal __________

(Answers are on page 263.)

Now it's time to learn a bit more about a special type of sentence ending—***quotation marks.***

Quotation Marks

You have learned a bit about this special sentence ending already. You know that when you write, you must use quotation marks to set apart a speaker's words from the rest of the sentence. You have seen how to use ***quotation marks*** at the beginning and the end of a direct quotation. A **direct quotation** is the exact words that someone said. The following is an example of a sentence containing a direct quotation.

Ms. Garcia said, "Your assignments are due today."

Notice that the quotation marks set off only the direct quotation, which in the above sentence is: *Your assignments are due today*. Also notice that the direct quotation is a **declarative sentence**, so the first letter is capitalized and as you learned earlier ends with a period. By contrast, let's look at the same direct quotation, but written in a slightly different form:

> "Your assignments are due today," Ms. Garcia said.

Here, the declaratory sentence direct quotation appears at the beginning, rather than at the end as in the previous example. In this form, the comma is inside the quotation marks, and the entire sentence ends with a period.

The following is another example of a direct quotation in this form:

> "I enjoy writing stories in English," Pham said.

Again, notice that the comma is inside the quotation marks, and the entire sentence ends with a period.

Let's look at a direct quotation that is an **interrogative sentence**:

> Carla asked, "Where should we put our assignments?"
> "Where do you usually put them?" asked Ms. Garcia.

Here, quotation marks enclose the direct quotation that is an interrogative sentence. Notice the position of the question mark and the ending quotation mark. The question mark is always on the <u>inside</u> of the ending quotation mark.

Finally, let's look at direct quotations that are **exclamatory sentences** and **imperative sentences**. As you learned, both of these types of sentences must end with an exclamation point. Here are examples of direct quotation that is an **exclamatory sentence**:

> Bonita screamed, "Our team won the championship!"
> "This is fantastic!" exclaimed Juan.

Now, the direct quotation that is an imperative sentence:

> Ugo shouted, "Don't run into the street!" (The subject *you* is understood.)
> "Stop!" screamed Isis.

As before, notice the position of the sentence ending, which here is an exclamation point and the ending quotation mark. Always write the exclamation point inside of the ending quotation mark.

Work through the following exercise to make sure that you can use ***quotation marks***.

BRAIN TICKLERS!
Set #2
MORE ABOUT DENTAL HEALTH

For each of the sentences, use ***quotation marks*** and other necessary ***sentence endings*** to correctly write the sentence on the line provided.

EXAMPLE:

Did you know that sugar is bad for your teeth asked Pham.

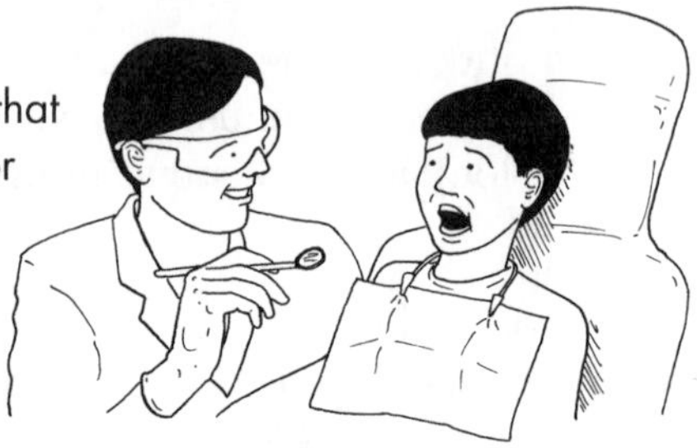

"Did you know that sugar is bad for your teeth**?"** asked Pham.

1. Pham asked Do you remember how we talked about bacteria forming plaque

   ____

2. Plaque can cause cavities I continued

   ____

3. The bacteria colony uses sugar for its food replied Pham

   ____

4. The bacteria multiply faster when they have more sugar available to them he said

   ____

5. He said Some of the bacteria turn the sugar into a kind of glue

   ____

6. Once it forms, the sticky plaque is hard for us to remove Pham said

   ____

7. He also said It is the acid formed underneath the plaque that eats a hole in the enamel of our teeth

   ____

8. What should we do to keep plaque off our teeth I asked

____

9. Pham said The dentist can use various techniques to remove the plaque and prevent cavities

____

10. I'm going to make a dental appointment today I exclaimed

____

(Answers are on page 263.)

This concludes the section on sentence endings, now let's learn about punctuation that helps you when you need ***pauses*** in your sentences.

SENTENCE PAUSES

When you write, there are five symbols to indicate a pause shorter than a period, and they are important to keep in mind because a sentence pause can add meaning, as well as, make your writing clearer. The five symbols to indicate a pause in a sentence shorter than a period are to use

- Commas
- Semicolons
- Colons
- Dashes
- Parentheses

Now you are ready to learn about each type of sentence pause. Let's start with the most commonly used punctuation mark to create a sentence pause—the ***comma***.

Commas

A ***comma (,)*** is the form of punctuation used to indicate a slight separation of information or a slight pause in the writing. The comma has many uses in the English language; however, its most common use is to **separate items in series**. A **series** is three or more related words, phrases, or clauses. The following are examples of commas separating items in a series.

Juan has a dog**,** a cat**,** and three goldfish. (series of words)
On the hill, next to the highway, and across from the stadium are different ways to describe the location of my school. (series of phrases)
Juan went to the movies, Marta stayed home and studied, and Carlos went fishing. (series of clauses)

IMPORTANT!

You should always have one less comma than the number of items in your series. In the following example, the writer has three sisters, and therefore, must use two commas.

I have three sisters: Marta, Carla, and Maria.

Another common use for a comma is to **separate two or more adjectives** that are written before a noun in a sentence.

Max is an old**,** friendly dog.
Ms. Garcia is a kind**,** intelligent woman.

In Chapter Four you learned about adjectives. Recall that a comma can be used to replace the word *and*. If the adjectives can be separated by the word *and*, then you can also use a comma to separate the adjectives. For instance, in the last example, you could have written:

Ms. Garcia is a *kind* <u>and</u> *intelligent* woman.

On the other hand, if your adjectives can't be separated by the word *and*, then don't use a comma. In other words, do not use a comma if the adjectives in front of the noun express a single idea.

<u>Incorrect</u>
I have two**,** younger sisters.

This sentence incorrectly uses a comma because if you insert the word *and* between the two adjectives *two* and *younger*, the sentence doesn't make any sense:

I have *two* and *younger* sisters.

This means the adjectives express a single idea; consequently, a comma isn't needed to separate them.

Another use for the comma is to separate the **simple sentences** that comprise a compound sentence.

Ugo and Pham play for the Wildcats, and I play for the Tigers.

In this example, our compound sentence is comprised of the two simple sentences: *Ugo and Pham play for the Wildcats* and *I play for the Tigers*. You must use a comma to separate these two simple sentences within the compound sentence.

Use a comma after an **introductory word, phrase,** or **clause** that you have written to begin the sentence.

Introductory Word
Oh, I didn't know you wanted to go with us.
Yes, I would like to go with you.

Introductory Phrase
During the day, most animals sleep.
Through the night, the animals hunt.

Introductory Clause
While I waited for the bus, I studied my vocabulary words.
Before the bus arrived, I had learned ten new words.

Use commas to separate **nouns of direct address** from the rest of the sentence. A **noun of direct address** is the name of a person or persons spoken to directly in the sentence. A noun of direct address can be written anywhere in the sentence, but you usually write it at the beginning of the sentence.

Juan, I want you to play goalie for us during the tournament.
Ugo, you have the highest grade in the class.
You have the second highest grade, *Maria.*

Use commas to separate an **appositive** from the rest of the words, but only if it is not necessary to identify the noun. An **appositive** adds information about the noun that directly precedes it.

Ms. Garcia, *our social studies teacher,* is taking us on a field trip.

Our starting goalie, *Juan*, twisted his ankle.

By contrast, in the following example, the appositive is necessary to identify the noun, so do not use commas to separate it from the rest of the sentence.

The movie *Tales from Outer Space* is playing at several local theaters.

Surf's up...

Here's a great site to help you understand when and how to use *commas* to create pauses in your sentences:

http://esl.about.com/od/englishgrammar/a/a_punctuation.htm

As you can see, the ***comma*** performs many functions in sentences. Work through the following exercise to practice using this powerful bit of punctuation.

BRAIN TICKLERS!
Set #3
CLARA BARTON—FOUNDER OF THE AMERICAN RED CROSS

For each of the sentences below, insert ***commas*** where they are needed. Remember how commas create a pause in your sentences by separating words, and the six ways they do this is to separate:

- Items in a series

- Two or more adjectives from one another
- Simple sentences in a compound sentence
- An introductory word, phrase, or clause from the rest of the sentence
- Nouns of direct address from the rest of the sentence
- An appositive from the rest of the sentence

On the line provided after each sentence, write the type of words the comma is separating.

EXAMPLE:

Roman do you know who started the Red Cross?

Roman, do you know who started the Red Cross?
noun of direct address

1. The Red Cross a special group that helps people during disasters is over 100 years old. __________
2. Clara Barton is the founder of the American Red Cross and she is champion of helping the less fortunate. __________
3. When she was eleven years old her brother was seriously injured. __________
4. While nursing him back to health she learned much about medicine and helping sick and injured people. __________
5. During the Civil War Clara raised money for medical supplies and transported them herself to the front lines. __________
6. Because she gave so much care to the wounded soldiers people began calling her the "Angel of the Battlefield." __________
7. This hard work took a toll on her and Clara became very sick. __________
8. To recover her health she went to Switzerland and stayed with friends. __________
9. While she was in Switzerland the founders of the International Red Cross asked her to start an American branch of the Red Cross. __________
10. The American Red Cross began in 1881 and Clara Barton served as its first president for twenty-three years. __________

(Answers are on page 264.)

Commas are a powerful piece of punctuation and can help you to write more clearly. Now, let's look at another form of punctuation that you can use to create a pause in sentences—the ***semicolon***.

Semicolons

A ***semicolon (;)*** presents a longer pause than the one provided by a comma. Consequently, semicolons are used for two special cases. The first case is to **separate two independent clauses** that have commas within one or both of them. The semicolon shows your reader where the complete thoughts begin and end, thus avoiding confusion. Notice how the semicolon creates a pause or break in the following sentence and, by doing so, makes it easier to read and understand.

> Santiago plays football, basketball, and baseball; and his sister plays soccer and volleyball.

In the above example, a semicolon separates two independent clauses. The first independent clause is *Santiago plays football, basketball, and baseball.* The other independent clause is *his sister plays soccer and volleyball.* Notice how the semicolon causes you to pause as you read the sentence, making it clearer as to the sports Santiago plays and the sports his sister plays.

> Our band is missing a flutist, a trombone player, and a French horn player; and our concert is less than a week away.

In the above sentence, can you identify the independent clauses separated by the semicolon? Remember: An independent clause contains a subject and a predicate and expresses a complete thought.

The second case where a semicolon creates a sentence pause is when it **separates two independent clauses** where the second clause begins with an adverb, such as *however, therefore, consequently, besides, moreover, furthermore*, or *nonetheless*.

> Our team practices every day; however, we have yet to win a game.
> It rained hard last night; consequently, the trails are very muddy.

You will use semicolons much less frequently than you will use commas, but semicolons are an important bit of punctuation. Consequently, when you use them correctly, your writing will appear very polished. Let's move on to the next punctuation mark that signals a pause in a sentence—the ***colon***.

Colons

A ***colon (:)*** is used to create a pause and then direct your reader's attention to what follows it. Use a colon before a **list of people, places,** or **things** in a sentence. The list may contain one or many people, places, or things. When you use words such as *the following* or *these*, you will want to follow them with a colon.

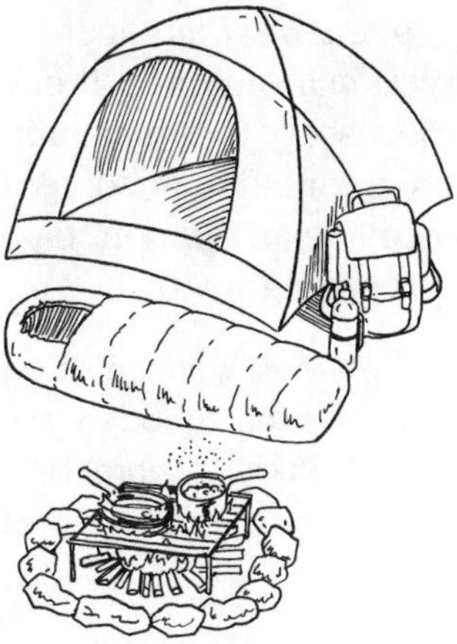

> In math class this year, we have studied the following: fractions, inequalities, and variables.
>
> On the next campout, bring these: sleeping bag, tent, food, and water.

Surf's up...

Glide into this site to learn more about *semicolons* and *colons*:

http://www.mun.ca/writingcentre/colonrules.sthml

Dashes

Use a ***dash*** (—) to set off a sudden change in the normal flow of your sentence.

This is the best hamburger that I have ever eaten—or so it seems.
The day we went to the aquarium—Friday March 24—was an unforgettable day.

Because the dash can add emphasis and character to your writing, don't use it too much, or it will lose its affect.

You are now ready to look at the final way to create a pause in your sentence, and that is with ***parentheses ( )***.

Parentheses

Parenthesis indicates another type of pause or interruption within a sentence. It encloses information that isn't absolutely necessary to the meaning of a sentence or information that may be interesting to some readers. For instance, parenthesis can provide an opinion, factual information, or a definition of a preceding word.

Most nutritionists agree that a small amount of chocolate (my favorite food) is actually good for you.
Students, parents, and teachers named Ms. Garcia (she teaches social studies) Teacher of the Year.

Surf's up...

If you want to learn more about using *dashes* or *parentheses* in your writing, check out this site:

http://owl.english.purdue.edu/handouts/grammar/g_overvw.html

You have now learned the five types of punctuation that you can use to create a pause within a sentence. Use the exercise below as a review of this important punctuation group.

BRAIN TICKLERS!
Set #4
PROTECTING OUR FORESTS

For each of the sentences below, rewrite the sentence on the line provided so that it correctly punctuates the sentence pauses with ***commas***, ***semicolons***, ***colons***, ***dashes***, or ***parentheses***.

EXAMPLE:

Deforestation which is the permanent destruction of forests harms everyone.

<u>Deforestation, which is the permanent destruction of forests, harms everyone.</u>

1. Deforestation is caused by the following: clearing the trees away to provide land for agriculture clearing the trees to create pasture land for cattle ranching and clearing away trees to make room for roads and houses.

   ____

2. The consequences of deforestation are the following global warming, soil erosion, and species extinction.

   ____

3. The *greenhouse effect* is a major cause of global warming and the greenhouse effect results from increasing amounts of carbon dioxide being released into the atmosphere.

___

4. Forests act as a "carbon dioxide sponge" by absorbing the carbon dioxide from the atmosphere and using it to produce the carbon-based nutrients, such as carbohydrates fats and proteins that make up trees.

___

5. Unfortunately when forests are cleared and the trees are either burnt or rot these carbon-based nutrients are released as carbon dioxide.

___

6. Scientists believe that deforestation the destruction of forests contributes more than one-third of the carbon dioxide released into the atmosphere.

___

7. Many animals more than half of the species on Earth depend upon forests for food and shelter.

___

8. After the trees in a particular area have been removed there is nothing to hold the soil in place.

___

9. As a result areas experience widespread *erosion.*

___

10. This erosion is harmful for the following reasons plants don't have enough soil for growth, the soil that has been eroded dumps into streams and kills the fish, and there is less soil to hold moisture.

___

(Answers are on page 264.)

Now that you have learned to punctuate sentences, let's move on to the next chapter and learn more about ***sentences*** and how to better write them.

CHAPTER TEN

Writing Sentences

In the preceding chapters, you learned about the **parts of speech** and how to **punctuate** sentences. Now it's time to take what you know about words and punctuation and elevate your English skills to the next level by writing better ***sentences***. You want to learn about sentences because sentences allow you to express yourself in complete, clear thoughts to readers. What's more, by writing a group of sentences, you can create a paragraph. Even better, by writing several paragraphs, you can create a composition, a story, or any variety of writings that helps you to communicate your thoughts in your new language. After all, that is what writing in any language is about: **Communicating your thoughts**. So, let's learn about sentences.

WHAT IS A SENTENCE?

As you have learned, a ***sentence*** is a group of words that contains a subject, a predicate, and expresses a complete thought. A sentence can either:

- State something
- Ask someone to do something
- Command someone to do something
- Exclaim something

For instance, the following group of words **states** something: the color of the sky.

The sky is blue.

This group of words is a sentence because it contains a subject **(the sky)** and a predicate **(is blue)** and expresses a complete thought by stating something.

The next group of words **commands** someone to do something.

John, be on time.

This group of words is a sentence because it contains a subject **(John),** a predicate **(be on time),** and expresses a complete thought by commanding its subject ***John*** to be on time.

These are examples of two kinds of sentences, and we'll look at other types just a bit later in the chapter. First, though, let's learn how we build sentences by using **subjects** and **predicates**.

SUBJECTS AND PREDICATES

The ***subject*** is the **noun** or **pronoun** and all the words that describe what the rest of the sentence is talking about. The rest of the sentence is called the ***predicate.*** It includes the **verb** and all the words in the sentence that tell you what the subject *is* or *is doing*. The groups of words below are sentences because they contain a subject, a predicate, and express a complete thought—the **subject** has a single underline; the **predicate**, a double underline.

The goalie caught the ball.
Linda and her mother went shopping.
Carlos correctly answered all of the questions on the test.

On the other hand, the following groups of words **are not** sentences:

Runs to the store
A big dog
Fell into the mud puddle

Why aren't they sentences? Let's look at the first example: *runs to the store*. This group of words isn't a sentence because it does not contain a **subject**. *Who* or *what* runs to the store? You don't know. The words don't tell you, so this isn't a sentence. What information does the next group of words provide? For instance, what is the big dog doing? You don't know because there is no **predicate** to tell you, so this isn't a sentence. Finally, let's look at *fell into the mud puddle*. Again, this is similar to the first group of words because there is no **subject** to tell you *who* or *what* fell into the mud puddle.

These previous groups of words are called **sentence fragments**. They are pieces or fragments of a sentence, not complete sentences, because they don't contain both a subject, and a predicate and do not express a complete thought.

Being able to recognize the difference between a sentence and a sentence fragment is necessary for writing clearly in English. Use the following exercise to practice telling the difference between ***sentences*** and ***sentence fragments***.

BRAIN TICKLERS!

Set #1

DISTINGUISHING BETWEEN SENTENCES AND SENTENCE FRAGMENTS

Below are some groups of words. First, decide if the group of words is a ***sentence*** or a ***sentence fragment*** and then write an "S" for sentence or "F" for fragment on the line provided. If the group of words is a sentence, single underline the subject and double underline the predicate.

EXAMPLE:

Pham is entering the classroom. **S**

In the corner. **F**

1. Bonita and J.R. were looking forward to Gina's party. ____
2. Roberto's father took him to the soccer game. ____
3. Inside the box was a prize. ____
4. On the side of the box. ____
5. She gave me a pair of scissors. ____
6. The scissors are on the desk. ____
7. The large, red apple. ____
8. It is I. ____
9. The planets revolve around the sun. ____
10. She hid behind the tree. ____

(Answers are on page 265.)

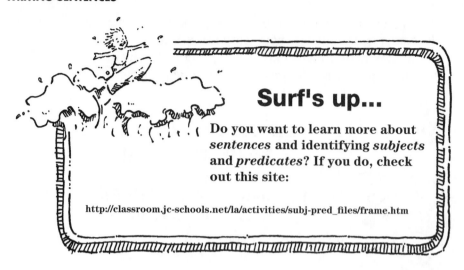

Surf's up...

Do you want to learn more about *sentences* and identifying *subjects* and *predicates*? If you do, check out this site:

http://classroom.jc-schools.net/la/activities/subj-pred_files/frame.htm

SUBJECT-PREDICATE AGREEMENT

One important way to write clear sentences is to make sure that the predicate **agrees** in number with its subject. ***Agreement*** means that a singular subject (noun or pronoun) requires a singular predicate (verb). As you would guess, a plural subject (noun) requires a plural predicate (verb). Let's see how to make subjects and predicates agree. As before, the **subject** in each sentence is single underlined, and the **verb** is double underlined.

Singular Subject/Singular Predicate

The dog jumps up and down.

Since **dog** is a singular subject, it needs a singular predicate verb **jumps**. Remember, **jumps** is a verb, and it ends with an ***–s*** because it is in the third person, not because it is plural.

The man runs across the street.

Here again, you have a singular subject *man*. It needs a singular predicate verb **runs** for the sentence to be correctly written.

Let's look at sentences with a plural subject.

Plural Subject/Plural Predicate

The dogs jump up and down.

The subject in this sentence **dogs** is plural. For subject-predicate agreement, you must use a plural predicate verb **jump**.

The men run across the street.

In this example, the subject **men** is plural. Consequently, you must use a plural predicate verb **run** so that your subject and predicate agree.

In sentences containing more than one subject, the word *and* usually appears between the subject nouns.

Mary *and* I are here.

A sentence written like this is said to have a **compound subject**, namely *Mary and I.* Compound subjects are plural subjects. To write sentences that have compound subjects correctly, you must use a plural predicate verb. Here, you should use the plural predicate verb **are**.

Incorrect
Reading the material and reviewing my notes helps me learn.

The sentence is incorrect because you have a plural subject **reading the material** and **reviewing my notes**, but the predicate verb **helps** is singular. To write the sentence correctly, you must use **help** as your predicate verb because it is plural.

Correct
Reading the material out loud and reviewing my notes help me learn.

Think of reading the material and reviewing my notes as They, so then the sentence becomes They **help** me learn.

Incorrect
A mother and her daughter waits for the bus.

As in the previous sentence, this sentence is incorrect because it has a plural subject **a mother and her daughter**, but the predicate verb **waits** is singular. To write the sentence correctly, you need to use a plural predicate verb **wait**.

Correct
A mother and her daughter wait for the bus.

Sometimes a phrase within a sentence makes the sentence appear to have a compound subject. Examples of these phrases that sometimes can confuse things are

accompanied by	*in addition to*
along with	*including*
as well as	*together with*

When you use one of these phrases in your sentence, you may be thinking of more than one person or thing. Nevertheless, these phrases aren't conjunctions like *and*. Instead, they are **describing** the subject, not making it compound. Therefore, do not use a plural verb.

Incorrect
Maria, *accompanied by* her sisters, are arriving by bus.

This sentence is grammatically incorrect because the subject of the sentence **Maria** is singular and needs a singular verb, but **are** is a plural verb. The phrase *accompanied by her sisters* merely describes the subject **Maria**.

Correct
Maria, *accompanied by* her sisters, is arriving by bus.

This sentence is now written correctly because it uses a singular predicate verb **is,** which agrees with the singular subject, **Maria**.

Incorrect
Ms. Smith, *along with* her class, are going on the field trip.

This sentence is grammatically incorrect because the subject of the sentence **Ms. Smith** is singular and needs a singular verb, but the writer has used a plural verb **are**. Don't be confused—the phrase *along with her class* merely describes the subject **Ms. Smith**; it is not part of the subject.

Correct
Ms. Smith, *along with* her class, is going on the field trip.

This sentence is now correctly written because it has a singular predicate verb **is**, which agrees with the singular subject, **Ms. Smith**.

Predicate Before the Subject

In most of your sentences, you will write the subject **before** the predicate, and that is the case for the sentences below. Once again, the subject is single underlined; the predicate, double underlined.

The dog chased the fire truck.
The cow jumped over the moon.
The astronomers discovered a new planet.

Although this subject-before-the-predicate order is more common, it isn't required. Consequently, you can write sentences with the subject appearing **after** the predicate. The following are examples of sentences written like this. As before, the subject is single underlined; the predicate, double underlined.

Behind the tree hides the dog.
Outside the classroom waits the teacher.
Near the goal crouches the goalie.

If you decide to write a subject after the predicate, be sure to check agreement between the subject and the verb in the predicate.

Incorrect
In the restaurant waits the chef and two of his helpers.

This sentence lacks subject and predicate agreement because it contains a plural subject **the chef and two of his helpers**, but the predicate verb **waits** is singular.

Correct
In the restaurant wait the chef and two of his helpers.

This sentence is correctly written because the subject and the verb agree. The subject **the chef and two of his helpers** is plural and so is the verb **wait**.

Incorrect
On top of the hill sits many students.

This sentence lacks subject and predicate agreement because it contains a plural subject **students**, but the predicate verb **sits** is singular.

Correct
On top of the hill sit many students.

This sentence is correctly written because the subject and verb agree. The subject **students** is plural and so is the verb **sit**.

Surf's up...

Glide into this site to learn more about *subject-predicate* agreement:

http://classroom.jc-schools.net/la/activities/verb-subjagree_files/v3_document.htm

Use the following exercise to help you make sure you have mastered ***subject-predicate*** agreement.

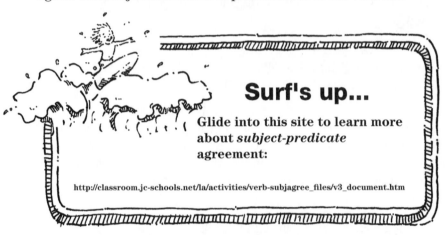

BRAIN TICKLERS!
Set #2
PROTECTING YOURSELF AGAINST THE SUN

For each of the sentences below, check for ***subject-verb agreement*** by single underlining the subject and double underlining the correct verb in each of the following sentences.

EXAMPLE

The sun, with its ultraviolet rays, (is, are) harmful to our skin and eyes.

1. Various types of cancers (is, are) caused by repeated exposure to the sun.
2. Damage, especially to the eyes, (is, are) a serious problem caused by too much exposure to the sun.
3. Exposure to the sun over a number of years (causes, cause) your skin to become dry and wrinkled.

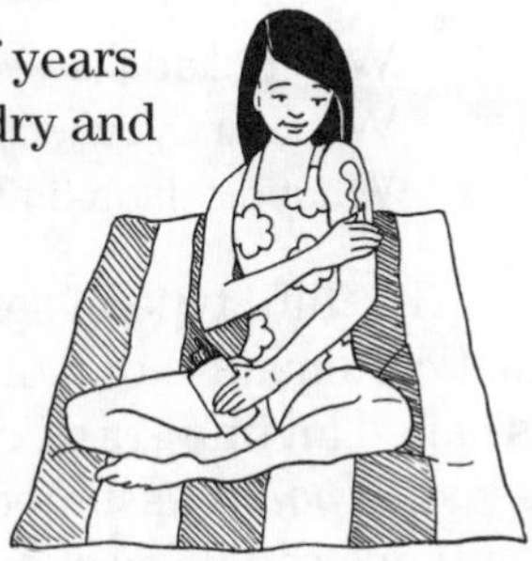

4. At what time (is, are) the sun and its ultraviolet rays the most dangerous?
5. Between 10:00 A.M. and 3:00 P.M., the sun's rays (is, are) the strongest.
6. A sunscreen with a *sun protection factor* (SPF) of 15 or higher (protects, protect) your skin.
7. All, especially a child, (needs, need) to wear sunscreen when they are outdoors in the sun.
8. Another good idea for all people (is, are) to wear a cap or hat when working or playing in the sun.
9. People with fair skin (is, are) at the greatest risk of skin cancer.
10. Nonetheless, even people with dark hair and dark skin (is, are) at risk for skin cancer.

(Answers are on page 266.)

TYPES OF SENTENCES

You can use sentences to communicate many things. Let's take a minute to review what you learned in Chapter Eight. Remember: If you write a sentence that states something, this kind of sentence is called a **declarative sentence**. All declarative sentences end with a period. Below are some examples of declarative sentences:

Sylvia baked a chocolate cake.
The ball sailed into the goal.
Juan found his book.

You can also write a sentence that asks a question. This kind of sentence is called an **interrogative sentence**. All interrogative sentences end with a question mark. Below are some examples of interrogative sentences:

Who baked the chocolate cake?
When are you leaving?
What did Juan find?

The third type of sentence that you can write is a sentence that commands someone to do something. This kind of sentence is called an **imperative sentence**. It appears to have no subject because *you* is assumed to be the subject. An imperative sentence can be as short as one word. Because they are forceful, imperative sentences end with exclamation points.

Get out of the way! (*You* get out of the way!)
Run! (*You* run!)

Finally, you can write a sentence that shows excitement or strong emotion. This kind of sentence is called an **exclamatory sentence**. As you learned in Chapter Eight, exclamatory sentences end with an exclamation point.

We scored the goal!
What a delicious cake!
Juan, watch out!

Surf's up...

Here is a good web site to help you learn more about the *declarative*, *interrogative*, *imperative*, and *exclamatory* sentences:

http://www.eslincanada.com/englishlesson2.html

Try the following exercise to make sure that you can identify ***declarative***, ***interrogative***, ***imperative***, and ***exclamatory*** sentences.

BRAIN TICKLERS!
Set #3
MORE ABOUT PROTECTING YOURSELF FROM THE SUN

Decide whether each of the following sentences is a **declarative, interrogative**, **exclamatory,** or an **imperative** sentence. Write the type of sentence on the line provided.

EXAMPLE:

Did you know that repeated exposure to the sun's ultraviolet rays can cause skin cancer?
interrogative

1. That's scary! ______________
2. You can enjoy the outdoors, but you have to be careful. ______________
3. You should also wear sunglasses to protect your eyes against the sun's ultraviolet rays. ______________
4. I think having a suntan makes a person look "healthy," don't you? ______________
5. No, because tanning means you might be getting too much sun. ______________
6. What if I use a sun lamp or a tanning bed to get a tan? ______________
7. They are very dangerous! ______________
8. They give off harmful ultraviolet rays, just like the sun. ______________
9. You should wear a hat and lightweight clothing when you are out in the sun, as well as cover exposed skin with a sunscreen. ______________
10. Cover up! ______________

(Answers are on page 266.)

You can identify the parts of a sentence and the types of sentences. Now it is time to use this knowledge to ***write sentences***.

WRITING SIMPLE SENTENCES

We've seen how sentences can

- State something
- Ask a question
- Command someone to do something
- Exclaim something

What's great about sentences is that they can be written in a variety of ways to accomplish all these things. Some of these sentences have rather simple structures, but you can also write some sentences that have more complicated structures. Let's look at the sentence:

The sky is blue.

This is a ***simple sentence*** because it contains one independent clause and no dependent clauses. An **independent clause** is a group of words that contains a subject and a predicate that can stand alone as a complete sentence. By contrast, a **dependent clause** is a group of words that contains a subject and a verb; however, it does not express a complete thought. Below are some examples of ***simple sentences***:

The teacher entered the classroom.
Nadia finished her homework.
The band left the stage.

You have seen what sentences look like and the different kinds of things they can do. Now it is your turn to write some ***simple sentences*** of your own. Remember: For a group of words to be a sentence, it must have a subject, a predicate, and express a complete thought. Finally, for a sentence to be a ***simple sentence*** it must contain only one independent clause and no dependent clauses.

BRAIN TICKLERS!

Set #4

WRITING SIMPLE SENTENCES

Write a ***simple sentence*** about each of these ideas on the line provided.

EXAMPLE:

Ms. Garcia and **Maria**

Ms. Garcia is helping **Maria** with a homework problem.

1. Juan and his dog
2. Someone asking directions
3. A new car
4. Carlos scoring a goal
5. Telling someone to meet you somewhere
6. Find out what kind of music Carla likes
7. Exclaim about the hot weather
8. Asking Linda to meet you at the mall
9. Find out what Tom is doing
10. Your favorite teacher

(Some suggested sentences are shown on page 266.)

Surf's up...

If you would like to know more about communicating through *sentences*, check out this site.

http://homeworktips.about.com/cs/grammar/a/sentences.htm

Choppy Writing

Read the paragraph below. Notice the type of sentences that it contains.

> I was hungry for a pizza. Janie wanted ice cream. We were hungry for different things. We decided to go to the mall. They have a food court there. I ate a huge piece of pepperoni pizza at the mall. Janie ate an ice cream cone with two scoops of ice cream at the mall.

Did you find this paragraph interesting? Did you want to read more?

The paragraph was not interesting because every one of its sentences is a simple sentence. Writing with only simple sentences creates what is called **choppy writing.** Choppy writing creates uninteresting paragraphs, and people will not like reading them. This is exactly the opposite of what you want to happen. You want your readers to enjoy reading what you have written. Although there is nothing grammatically wrong with short, simple sentences, they often separate ideas that should be brought together. That is why, to become a good writer, you must be able to write more than the simple sentence.

You can avoid writing with a choppy style by **varying** the types of sentences that you use. ***Sentence variation*** creates well-balanced, smooth writing that flows, making it easier and more interesting for someone to read.

BEYOND THE SIMPLE SENTENCE

As you read earlier, good writing requires that sometimes you express more than one thought or describe more than one action in a sentence. This means, to be a good writer, you have to be able to write more than simple sentences. Let's look at another type of sentence that can help your writing.

A ***compound sentence*** contains two or more independent clauses, but no dependent clauses. Notice in the following examples of compound sentences how a **comma** and a **coordinating conjunction** join the independent clauses (double underline) or a **semicolon** joins the clauses.

> I went to John's house, *but* he was not home.
> Carlos studied all night, *yet* he failed the test.
> The band performed on Tuesday, *but* their Wednesday performance was canceled.
> Juan has lived in the United States for five years; Maria has been here for four.

In addition to compound sentences, complex sentences provide you with another way to express multiple thoughts and actions, which will make your writing more interesting. A ***complex sentence*** is a sentence that includes one independent clause and one or more dependent clauses. Notice how a **comma** separates the dependent clause (single underline) from the independent clause (double underline).

> Since she enjoys writing, Juanita keeps a journal.
> To improve your writing, you should read books suggested by your teacher.
> Because he was in good physical condition, Carlos could easily run up and down the field.

Finally, the sentence that allows you to express the most complicated thoughts and actions is the compound-complex sentence. The ***compound-complex sentence*** contains two or more independent clauses and at least one dependent clause. Notice (1) how a **comma** separates the dependent clause (single underline) from the independent clauses (double underline) and (2) how the independent clauses are linked by a **coordinating conjunction**, *and*.

While Matt was sleeping, his parents decorated the house for his birthday *and* his sister baked him a cake.
Before Juan celebrated his birthday, his mother drove him to school in the morning *and* his grandmother picked him up in the afternoon.

The following exercise will give you a chance to identify ***simple sentences***, ***compound sentences***, ***complex sentences***, and ***compound-complex sentences***.

BRAIN TICKLERS!
Set #5
TAKING CARE OF YOUR PET

Decide whether each of the following sentences is a ***simple sentence***, a ***compound sentence***, a ***complex sentence,*** or a ***compound-complex sentence***. Write your answer on the line provided.

EXAMPLE:

Before you buy a pet, it is important for you to learn what you will have to do to take care of it.
complex sentence

1. You should know what kind of food to feed you pet, and you should know how often to feed it. ______________
2. You can ask your veterinarian, or you can ask someone who works at a pet store. ______________
3. A *veterinarian* is a doctor for animals. ______________
4. Don't feed you pet table scraps because people food usually makes most animals sick. ______________
5. Dogs and cats need to be fed once or twice a day. ______________

6. If you have a puppy or a kitten, you will have to feed it several times a day for a while. ______________
7. Make sure your pet has plenty of clean, fresh water. ______________
8. If your pet is a fish or a turtle and it lives in water, make sure to clean the tank at least once a week. ______________
9. If you own a dog, you need to spend time every day walking and playing with it because dogs need plenty of physical activity to stay healthy. ______________
10. Just like we need annual medical checkups, your pet needs to see the veterinarian at least once a year. ______________

(Answers are on page 266.)

Surf's up...

Surf into these sites for more information about *simple*, *compound*, *complex*, and *compound-complex* sentences.

http://www.eslbee.com/sentences.htm

http://www.evergreen.edu/writingcenter/handouts/grammar/compoundcomplex.pdf

MORE SENTENCE WRITING

Your writing will really flow when you mix some of the more complicated types of sentences with simple sentences. The following exercise will give you a chance to practice writing ***different types of sentences***.

BRAIN TICKLERS!

Set #6

MORE ABOUT OWNING A PET

Rewrite the information provided using the type of sentence shown in the parentheses.

EXAMPLE:

(complex sentence) A pet is fun. Many people want to own one.

Because a pet is fun, many people want to own one.

1. **(compound)** Owning a pet is a lot of fun. It is also a lot of work.

   ____

2. **(complex)** Pets cannot take care of themselves. You must help with their care.

   ____

3. **(compound-complex)** At least once a month. Luis gives his dog a bath. He cleans out the doghouse.

   ____

4. **(complex)** At least once a day. You should play with your pet every day, although you may busy studying or doing other things.

   ____

5. **(compound-complex)** While you are at school. Your pet needs to have food to eat. It also needs water to drink.

____

6. **(complex)** Your dog cannot get its own food and water. You must make sure to provide the food and water.

____

7. **(complex)** Make sure your pet is part of the family. You and the rest of your family must agree on rules for its behavior.

____

8. **(compound-complex)** As soon as you bring it home, you should begin teaching your puppy or dog. Your other family members should also help train your puppy or dog.

____

9. **(compound-complex)** While your dog may want it. Never feed your dog chocolate candy. Never feed your dog anything with chocolate in it.

____

10. **(complex)** A dog cannot digest chocolate. It can kill it if it eats too much.

____

(Suggested sentences are on page 267.)

Using a variety of sentences will make your writing easier to understand and more interesting. Every time you write something, you should think not only about the rules of grammar and vocabulary but about sentence structure as well. Let's see how the paragraph of **choppy writing** that you read earlier in this chapter can be improved by writing it with a variety of types of sentences.

Writing with Simple Sentences Only

I was hungry for a pizza. Janie wanted ice cream. We were hungry for different things. We decided to go to the mall. They have a food court there. I ate a huge piece of pepperoni pizza at the mall. Janie ate an ice cream cone with two scoops of ice cream at the mall.

Writing with a Variety of Types of Sentences

I was hungry for pizza, but Janie wanted ice cream. Since we were hungry for different things, we decided to go to the mall because they have a food court there. While we were at the mall, I ate a huge piece of pepperoni pizza, and Janie ate an ice cream cone with two scoops of ice cream.

You have learned how to avoid and fix choppy writing. Let's look at another problem encountered by many writers.

WATCH OUT FOR RUN-ONS!

As you know, choppy writing creates problems, but the other extreme—the run-on sentence—also hurts your writing. A ***run-on sentence*** is a sentence that contains either (1) two complete sentences separated by only a comma **(comma splice)** or (2) two complete sentences connected without any punctuation **(fused sentences)**. Run-on sentences occur because the writer wants to express more than one thought or action, but he or she uses incorrect punctuation, creating a confusing group of words. Below are examples where the writer has created run-on sentences by a **comma splice**:

Your sister is sleeping, talk softly.
Bonita keeps failing, she keeps trying.
We were lost, Pham could not read the map.

The above sentences can be corrected as follows:

Your sister is sleeping, **so** talk softly.
Bonita keeps failing, **but** she keeps trying.
We were lost **because** Pham could not read the map.

The following are examples of run-on sentences where the writer has **fused** two sentences. That is, the two sentences are not separated by any punctuation:

You ate too fast your stomach will hurt.
Luis said we passed the park I think it's farther ahead.
My family is excited about our vacation trip we're leaving tomorrow morning.

An independent clause standing alone should end in a period, question mark, or exclamation point. If you want to join independent clauses, you must insert a **semicolon** or a **comma** along with one of the seven **coordinating conjunctions** (*and*, *but*, *for*, *nor*, *or*, *so*, and *yet*) between them. Remember: A comma without the coordinating conjunction is not enough. Let's see how to improve the above run-on sentences.

Incorrect
You ate too fast now your stomach hurts.

Correct
You ate too fast, so now your stomach hurts.

Notice how the writer used a comma and the coordinating conjunction *so* to write a compound sentence.

Incorrect
Luis said we passed the park I think it's over there.

Correct
Luis said we passed the park, but I think it's over there.

Here, you can use a comma and the coordinating conjunction *but* to correct the run-on sentence and write a compound sentence.

Incorrect
My family is excited about our vacation trip we're leaving tomorrow morning.

Correct
My family is excited about our vacation trip; we're leaving tomorrow.

Notice how you can correct this run-on sentence by using a semicolon to write a compound sentence.

More Run-on Problems

Watch out for a run-on sentence created another way. You have learned that the only time you can join independent clauses with a comma is when you use a comma along with one of the seven coordinating conjunctions. Unfortunately, some words look like coordinating conjunctions, but aren't. These words that look like coordinating conjunctions are actually adverbs called

conjunctive adverbs. Using a comma with one of these words creates a run-on sentence. Here are a few of the conjunctive adverbs to watch out for:

also
besides
consequently
further
hence
however
indeed
likewise
moreover
nevertheless
otherwise
similarly
then
therefore
thus

Incorrect
The students enjoyed reading the story, however, their teacher did not enjoy it.

This is a run-on sentence because a comma and the conjunctive adverb *however* incorrectly connect the two independent clauses.

Correct
The students enjoyed reading the story; however, their teacher did not enjoy it.

Here you can correct the run-on sentence by using a **semicolon** to connect the independent clauses.

Surf's up...

Glide into this site if you want to learn more about recognizing and correcting *run-on sentences*:

http://www.ccc.commnet.edu/sensen/part2/nine/index.html

Use this next exercise to help you make sure you can identify and correct a ***run-on sentence***.

BRAIN TICKLERS!
Set #7
FLOWERING TREES

Decide which sentences are ***run-on sentences*** and which sentences are correct as written. Write **"RO"** in the blank provided if the sentence is a run-on. Write **"S"** in the blank provided if the sentence is correct as written. Next, fix the run-on sentences by using a **comma** and a **coordinating conjunction** (*but, or, yet, for, and, nor, so*) or by using a **semicolon** to separate the independent clauses.

EXAMPLE:

Most trees bloom in the spring, others bloom in late winter. **RO**

Most trees bloom in the spring, but others bloom in late winter.

1. Sometimes, trees bloom when something goes wrong in their environment. ____

   ____

2. If a tree is battered by a hurricane all of its leaves are stripped off, it may flower again although it is not spring. ____

   ____

3. During mild winters, trees flower early, if snow and ice come after the flowers are out, the flowers will die. ____

   ____

4. When it warms up again, the trees may start growing leaves, they may not be able to produce fruit. ____

   ____

5. *Pollen* is a fine golden dust from flowers. ____

____

6. For a flower to make seed, pollen from the male part (the *stamens*) must reach the female part (the *pistil*). ____

____

7. We call this process *pollination*. ____

____

8. Some tree types have male and female flowers on the same tree other types of trees have only female flowers or male flowers.____

____

9. All trees have flowers, it is the flowers that make the seeds. ____

____

10. A tree needs insects, birds, or bats to carry the tree's flower pollen to other flowers. ____

____

(Some possible answers are on page 267.)

Now it's time to take what you have learned about words, punctuation, and sentences and learn how to better write ***essays*** and ***stories***.

CHAPTER ELEVEN

Writing Essays and Stories

As you read in previous chapters, you can use the "building block" words of the earlier chapters to construct sentences. In this chapter, first, you will learn how to use sentences to create paragraphs that will help you focus your reader's attention on a topic. Then you will also see how to link paragraphs together to create essays and stories. Let's begin by learning how to use sentences to write paragraphs.

WHAT IS A PARAGRAPH?

If you think about it, when you write something, you want to inform, persuade, or entertain your reader, or maybe all three. No matter what you are writing, you need to present your thoughts in a logical manner in a series of paragraphs. A ***paragraph*** is a distinct division of your writing that begins on a new indented line, consists of one or more sentences, and deals with a single thought or topic. The purpose of the paragraph is to break up what you are writing into readable "chunks" because our brains process ideas in chunks. In fact, you are reading a paragraph.

WRITING PARAGRAPHS

To write an effective paragraph, each sentence must relate to the same single topic. To make this job easier, every paragraph should follow this basic form:

1. Begin each paragraph with a ***topic sentence***.
2. Follow it with ***support sentences*** that develop the topic sentence.
3. End each paragraph with a ***summarizing sentence***.

Let's look at each of the parts of a paragraph.

The Topic Sentence

The ***topic sentence*** is the paragraph's first and most important sentence, and its job is to tell the reader what the paragraph will be about. In other words, the topic sentence introduces the main idea of the paragraph. The sentence must be informative, but you don't want to or need to tell everything in the first sentence. Read the following short essay; the topic sentences are in bold.

Computer Viruses

Computer viruses are called "viruses" because they share some of the same traits as biological viruses. *A biological virus is not alive; consequently, the virus must inject its information or DNA into a living cell to, among other things, bring itself to life. Once it has done so, the virus's DNA then uses the healthy cell's systems to reproduce itself. Similarly, a computer virus also does this by using some other program or document in a "healthy" computer to activate itself, and to reproduce itself as well.*

Viruses are programmed not only to reproduce themselves but also to damage "host" files onto which they attach. *Consequently, it is this damage they cause that makes them dangerous. For instance, viruses can spread through e-mails and downloaded programs. Once the e-mail is opened or the downloaded program is installed, it attaches to files within your computer and can destroy your files without you even being aware of it. If you are not careful how you use your computer, viruses can damage your operating system and files to such a degree that it cannot be repaired.*

Protecting your computer's operating system and files can be accomplished in a number of ways. *The first way is to limit the number and type of programs that you download. Second, you can delete without opening e-mails from people who you don't know. Finally, you can install a virus protection program on your computer's operating systems. Together, these three methods can help protect your computer's operating system and its files from damage caused by viruses.*

Notice how the topic sentence in each paragraph presents the main idea of the paragraph. In the first paragraph, the main idea is that computer viruses and biological viruses are similar. Whereas, the second paragraph discusses that viruses can cause damage to your computer. Finally, the third paragraph explains how to keep viruses in check and protect your computer from damage.

Now that you understand topic sentences, let's move on to the rest of the paragraph.

Support Sentences

The next step is to follow the topic sentence with ***support sentences*** that develop the topic sentence. As you noticed in the essay on computer viruses, the topic sentence in each paragraph informs the reader what the rest of the paragraph will be talking about. That means the rest of the sentences must relate to and support the topic sentence in a logical manner. This is known as **paragraph unity**. A paragraph has unity when every sentence develops the idea mentioned in the topic sentence. To test the unity of your paragraph, read the support sentences. Are they developing the topic sentence or are they wandering off in another direction? Write each sentence with the previous one in mind. If the paragraph begins with one main idea, it should not end with another or introduce different ideas within the paragraph.

Let's examine the first paragraph of the computer virus essay for unity. Notice how the writer provides details to support the topic sentence. Research is necessary because these details are the result of research by the writer. Did you also notice how the sentences "flow" from one to the next in a logical order? This flowing logical structure makes the writing easier to read and understand.

Paragraph with Paragraph Unity

Computer viruses are called "viruses" because they share some of the same traits as biological viruses. A biological virus is not alive; consequently, the virus must inject its information or DNA into a living cell to, among other things, bring itself to life. Once it has done so, the virus's DNA then uses the healthy cell's systems to reproduce itself. Similarly, a computer virus also does this by using some other program or document in a "healthy" computer to activate itself, and to reproduce itself as well.

Notice how these sentences relate computer viruses to biological viruses, and by so doing support the topic sentence. Now let's read a paragraph that lacks paragraph unity. Notice how difficult it is to determine the writer's main point for the paragraph.

Paragraph Lacking Paragraph Unity

Computer viruses are called "viruses" because they share some of the same traits as biological viruses. Almost every one owns a computer because the cost of a computer has dropped over the past ten years. Computers are used in the home, at school, and in the workplace. A computer virus uses program files or documents within a "healthy" computer to activate itself and reproduce itself.

You've read how to write topic sentences and supporting sentences; all that is left for you to do is to end the paragraph. Let's see how to do this.

Summarizing Sentences

Finally, you should end each paragraph with a ***summarizing sentence***. A summarizing sentence should accomplish two things:

1. Restate the topic of the paragraph in different words than the topic sentence.
2. Provide a transition or "hook" to your next paragraph.

Let's look at the computer viruses essay again. The summarizing sentence in each paragraph is in **bold**.

Computer Viruses

Computer viruses are called "viruses" because they share some of the same traits as biological viruses. A biological virus is not alive; consequently, the virus must inject its information or DNA into a living cell to, among other things, bring itself to life. Once it has done so, the virus's DNA then uses the healthy cell's systems to reproduce itself. ***Similarly, a computer virus also does***

this by using some other program or document in a "healthy" computer to activate itself, and to reproduce itself as well.

Viruses are programmed not only to reproduce themselves but also to damage "host" files onto which they attach. Consequently, it is this damage they cause that makes them dangerous. For instance, viruses can spread through e-mails and downloaded programs. Once the e-mail is opened or the downloaded program is installed, it attaches to files within your computer and can destroy your files without you even being aware of it. ***If you are not careful how you use your computer, viruses can damage your operating system and files to such a degree that it cannot be repaired.***

Protecting your computer's operating system and files can be accomplished in a number of ways. The first way is to limit the number and type of programs that you download. Second, you can delete without opening e-mails from people who you don't know. Finally, you can install a virus protection program on your computer's operating systems. ***Together, these three methods can help protect your computer's operating system and its files from damage caused by viruses.***

Notice how the summarizing sentences of each paragraph restate the topic of the paragraph and provide a transition to the next paragraph. Now it is your turn to take what you have just learned and use the following exercise to practice writing a ***paragraph***.

BRAIN TICKLERS!

Set #1

TAKING CARE OF A PET

Use your own personal experience and the information provided in Chapter Nine, Exercise Sets #5 and #6 to write a ***paragraph*** (five to seven sentences in length) about owning a pet on the lines provided below. Be sure to include a ***topic***

sentence, support sentences, and a ***summarizing sentence***.

(A possible paragraph is on page 268.)

Now that you have learned to better write paragraphs, you can apply your skill to the types of writing that you will be asked to do.

ESSAYS AND STORIES

As a student, your writing will be one of two types. The first type of writing is the ***essay***. When you write an essay, you are usually doing one of the following:

- Describing a person, place, or thing
- Stating your opinion about a certain topic
- Analyzing something

The second type of writing is the ***story***, which is writing about something that happened or something that you have made up. Whether you are writing an essay or a story, the structure of the writing is the same.

THE STRUCTURE OF ESSAYS AND STORIES

Generally, both essays and stories consist of three parts: the ***introduction***, the ***body***, and the ***conclusion***. Notice that the structure of an essay or a story has the same structure as the paragraphs that comprise it. First, let's look at the introduction.

The Introduction

The ***introduction*** is the first section of your essay or story. It can consist of one or more paragraphs. This makes it extremely important because it is what your reader will use to decide if he or she wants to keep reading what you have written. It consists of two parts:

1. A **thesis statement** that summarizes the essay or story (The thesis statement also acts as a topic sentence for the first paragraph.)
2. A supporting sentence to attract your reader's attention

The Body

The ***body*** is the longest section of your essay or story. It consists of several supporting paragraphs that can cover several pages. Each of the paragraphs within the body must relate to the thesis statement, and each paragraph must follow the form and rules discussed in the previous section on paragraphs.

The Conclusion

The ***conclusion*** is the last part of your essay or story. If you are writing an essay, the conclusion summarizes your essay and restates in slightly different wording your thesis statement. By contrast, if you are writing a story, the conclusion brings the story to an end.

Now that you have seen the structure of what you will be writing, let's look at how you will go about writing essays and stories.

THE WRITING PROCESS

1. Select a topic

If your teacher didn't assign a topic to you, then you must select a topic. If you are allowed to select your topic, you will want to keep the following in mind:

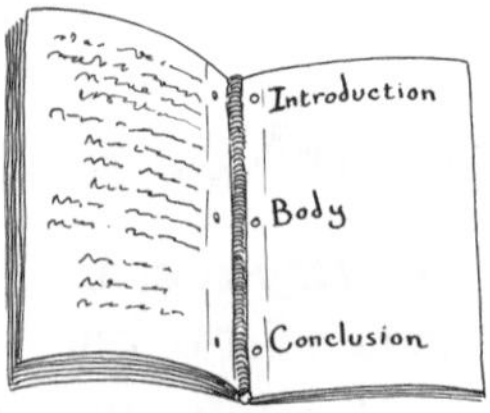

- Know how long your essay or story is supposed to be
- Understand your topic and the purpose for your writing (Decide what purpose you want to accomplish by writing about it. Is it to entertain? To inform? To persuade? Once you have decided upon your purpose, then your thinking, planning, and research should be aimed at achieving that purpose.)
- Make sure you have enough materials to write about your subject adequately

Once you have done the above, then you can move on to the next step.

2. Do your research

Explore ideas about the topic through thinking, reading, listening, and so on. Use the books and periodicals at your school's library and at the public library. You can also use the Internet, but don't use the information from any web site unless the site mentions its source of information. Keep a good record of the materials so that you can refer back to them, if necessary. If you are writing a story, use your personal experiences as well as research.

3. Write a thesis statement about your topic

As you read in the earlier section, the thesis statement should be part of your introduction. Writing a thesis statement based on your purpose for writing will focus your research and thinking, as well as provide direction for your essay or story. If you cannot explain your proposed topic in one sentence, you probably do not have a clear idea of what you want to write about. Below is the thesis statement for the computer viruses essay. Notice how the rest of the essay supports its thesis statement.

> Computer viruses are called "viruses" because they share some of the same traits as biological viruses.

The thesis statement is an important step in the writing process; do not change a well-thought-out thesis statement because you have not done sufficient research to support it. Go back, and do your research.

4. Develop an outline

So far, you have done some preliminary research and some thinking about your topic so that you can write a thesis statement. Once you have written your thesis statement, start making an outline containing main points that will comprise each of the body paragraphs and support the thesis statement. Decide on the order in which you'll present your ideas and examples.

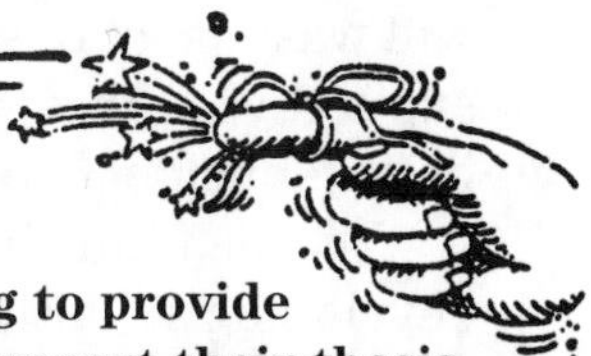

IMPORTANT!

A frequent mistake students make is failing to provide specific examples, evidence, or details to support their thesis statement.

If you are writing an essay, try to write three points to support your thesis statement. Assign each point its own section in the outline, keeping in mind that each supporting paragraph must support the thesis statement. Below is the outline for the computer viruses essay.

Outline for Computer Viruses Essay

I. Computer viruses are called "viruses" because they share some traits of biological viruses.
- **A. A biological virus injects its information into a living cell.**
- **B. A computer virus injects its information into a "healthy" computer.**

II. Viruses are programmed not only to reproduce themselves but also to damage "host" files onto which they attach.
   A. Viruses spread through e-mails and downloaded programs.
   B. Files can be destroyed.

III. Protecting your computer's operating system and files can be accomplished in a number of ways.
   A. Limit download programs.
   B. Don't open certain e-mails.
   C. Install a virus protection program.

Once you have completed your outline, you can use it as a framework for structuring your essay or story. From the above outline on computer viruses, each Roman numeral represents a paragraph, and each capital letter represents an idea that supports the topic of that paragraph.

Outlining is an important part of the writing process. Many students mistakenly believe that they can skip this process to save work. Yet, doing so will cost you more work because you will waste a lot of effort writing and researching things that don't support your thesis statement. As with the thesis statement, don't let inadequate research force you to change your outline.

Try the following exercise to give yourself some practice developing an outline.

BRAIN TICKLERS!
Set #2
CITY MAYORS

In this exercise you will work backwards so that you can see what can be written from an outline. In the space provided after the essay, write the major outline points of the essay.

City Mayors

The mayor of a large city is responsible for the executive and administrative duties in the city government. These duties include working with city council, overseeing how the police and fire departments are run, and making sure the city is prepared for an emergency, such as a hurricane, snowstorm, or terrorist attack. Because these duties are so numerous and complex, the mayor may not work at another job while he or she is mayor.

Since mayors must perform a number of important jobs, the citizens of the city want a say in who will serve as their mayor. The residents of the city elect their mayor through a citywide election. The mayor is elected to serve for a term of four years. Most cities allow a person, if reelected in the next election, to be a mayor for up to two terms, which is eight years.

City Mayors

I. ______________________________

A. ______________________________

B. ______________________________

II. ______________________________

A. ______________________________

B. ______________________________

C. ______________________________

(A possible outline is on page 268.)

Now that you had some practice developing an outline, let's continue learning about the writing process.

5. Write a first draft

Review what you have learned about writing sentences and paragraphs from the previous chapters. When writing the first draft, don't worry too much about grammar and punctuation—you can fix that in later drafts.

6. Edit and re-write your drafts until you have a final version

Often the act of writing itself generates new ideas you may want to pursue. The most realistic way to view writing is not as a straight line but as a back-and-forward movement. Continue writing until you feel you have accomplished the purpose of your writing. Once you have done so, check your grammar and spelling.

BRAIN TICKLERS!

Set #3

WRITING AN ESSAY

Use the information provided in some of the exercises, as well as from your own research, to write a three-paragraph essay on a topic of your choice. Develop a thesis statement, an outline, and finally the finished essay. This will provide you the opportunity to work through the entire writing process. Practice on this short essay will help you when you have to write a longer essay in school.

Topic:

Thesis Statement:

Outline:

Write your outline on a separate sheet of paper.

Essay:

Write your essay on a separate sheet(s) of paper.

(A sample structure is on page 268.)

PLAGIARISM

Plagiarism is inserting information directly as it is written from a book, magazine article, or web site into your essay or story without giving credit to its author. When you do this, you give the reader the impression that these are your thoughts, rather than those of the author. Plagiarism is wrong, and you will earn a bad grade from your teacher if you do it.

You have learned the structure for paragraphs, stories, and essays. In addition, you've seen and practiced the process for writing. Keep practicing these and use them every time you have to write a story or an essay. Everyone will be amazed at how much you have improved your writing.

IT'S UP TO YOU

You now have the knowledge to speak and write English better. Keep this book with you in case you have a question or problem concerning English. However, do not just refer to this book whenever you have a question or problem, also use it regularly to review what you have learned here. As you read in the Introduction, learning to speak and read English is a lifetime challenge. It is a fun and worthwhile challenge that requires work and patience. Good luck!

APPENDIX—THE AMERICAN HERITAGE COLLEGE DICTIONARY PRONUNCIATION GUIDE

1.	ă	p**a**t
2.	ā	p**ay**
3.	âr	**care**
4.	ä	f**a**ther
5.	b	**bib**
6.	ch	**church**
7.	d	**deed**, mille**d**
8.	ĕ	p**e**t
9.	ē	b**ee**
10.	f	**fif**e, **ph**ase, rou**gh**
11.	g	**gag**
12.	h	**h**at
13.	hw	**wh**ich
14.	ĭ	p**i**t
15.	ī	p**ie**
16.	îr	p**ier**
17.	j	**j**u**dg**e
18.	k	**k**i**ck**, **c**at, pi**que**
19.	l	**l**id, need**le**
20.	m	**mum**
21.	n	**n**o, sudd**en**
22.	ng	thi**ng**
23.	ŏ	p**o**t
24.	ō	t**oe**
25.	ô	c**augh**t, p**aw**, f**or**, h**o**rrid, h**oa**rse
26.	oi	n**oi**se
27.	o͝o	t**oo**k
28.	o͞o	b**oo**t
29.	ou	**ou**t
30.	p	**pop**
31.	r	**r**oa**r**
32.	s	**s**au**ce**
33.	sh	**sh**ip
34.	t	**t**igh**t**
35.	th	**th**in
36.	*th*	**th**is
37.	ŭ	c**u**t
38.	ûr	**ur**ge, t**er**m, f**ir**m, w**or**d, h**ear**d
39.	v	**v**al**v**e
40.	w	**w**ith
41.	y	**y**es
42.	z	**z**ebra, **x**ylem
43.	zh	vi**s**ion, plea**s**ure, gara**ge**
44.	ə	**a**bout, it**e**m, **e**dible, gall**o**p, circ**u**s
45.	ər	butt**er**

APPENDIX—FURTHER READING

Aitchison, James. *The Cassell Guide to Written English.* New York: Sterling Publishing, 1999.

Axlerod, Rise, and Charles Cooper. *The St. Martin's Guide to Writing*, Fifth Edition. New York: St. Martin's Press, 1997.

Eggenschwiler, Jean. *Writing: Grammar, Usage, and Style.* Lincoln: Cliffs Notes, Inc., 1997.

Fogiel, Max. *Handbook of English Grammar, Style and Writing.* Piscataway: Research & Education Association, 2003.

Fulwiler, Toby, and Allan Hayakawa. *The Blair Handbook*, Second Edition. Upper Saddle River: Blair Press, 1997.

Good, C. Edward. *Whose Grammar Is This Anyway?* New York: Barnes & Noble Books, 2002.

Greenbaum, Sidney. *A College Grammar of English.* New York: Longman, Inc., 1989.

Hahn, Pamela Rice, and Dennis E. Hensley. *Teach Yourself Grammar and Style in 24 Hours.* Indianapolis: Pearson Education Macmillan USA, 2000.

Hairston, Maxine, and John Ruskiewcz. *The Scott, Foresman Handbook for Writers*, Second Edition. New York: HarperCollins Publishers, 1991.

Haley-James, Shirley, and John Warren Stewig. *English: Your Communications Resource.* Boston: Houghton Mifflin Company, 1998.

Kemper, Dave. *Writers Express.* Burlington: Write Source Educational Publishing House, 1995.

Podhaizer, Mary Elizabeth. *Painless Spelling.* Hauppauge: Barron's Educational Series, Inc., 1998.

Strausser, Jeffrey. *Painless Writing.* Hauppauge: Barron's Educational Series, Inc., 2001.

Williams, Joseph. *Style: Toward Clarity and Grace.* Chicago: The University of Chicago Press, 1990.

ANSWER KEY

CHAPTER ONE: NOUNS

Set #1, page 6—Reading and Writing in English

1. Ms. Garcia, teacher
2. United States, years
3. Reading, skill
4. stories, world
5. reader, English
6. stories, English
7. Reading, writing, English, time, work
8. time, day, words, words, sentences
9. words, sentences, notebook
10. week, story, notebook, computer

Set #2, page 7—The British Colonies in 18th-Century America

1. land, home, Europeans
2. Africans, Native Americans
3. Historians, area, regions
4. Massachusetts, Connecticut, Rhode Island, New Hampshire, colonies, New England
5. Fishing, source, money, towns, Atlantic Ocean
6. society, area, states, Pennsylvania, Delaware, New Jersey, New York
7. settlers, farmers, soil, region
8. colonies, Virginia, Maryland, North Carolina, South Carolina, Georgia
9. climate, tobacco, rice
10. Merchants, England, Germany, Spain, crops

Set #3, page 10—Citizenship

1. Honesty, responsibility, traits, citizen

C C
2. Honesty, people, cultures

C
3. culture
4. language, customs, religion

C C C
5. group, group people, customs

C
6. Responsibility, problems, society
7. school, rules, responsibility

C
8. United States, *democracy*

C
9. Citizens, democracy, representatives

C
10. Education, citizens, voters, problems, society

Set #4, page 13—Frequently Used Nouns

1. churches
2. flowers
3. wishes
4. birthdays
5. days
6. words
7. houses
8. speeches
9. families
10. schools

Set #5, page 15—More Frequently Used Nouns

1. tomatoes
2. knives
3. halves
4. mice
5. rodeos
6. leaves
7. thieves
8. men
9. radios
10. selves

Set #6, page 17—Frequently Used Possessive Nouns

1. tigers'
2. tree's
3. Ms. Jones'
4. thief's
5. thieves'
6. leaf's
7. leaves'
8. teachers'
9. baker's
10. Maria's

Set #7, page 20—Using Possessive Nouns

1. **C**
2. **I**, Let's go over to John and Sally's house.
3. **I**, Bill's and Obi's pants are blue.
4. **I**, The Tigers' and the Lions' uniforms look similar.
5. **I**, Ms. Jones', Mr. Clark's, and Ms. Kelly's classes were cancelled.
6. **C**
7. **C**
8. **I**, Roberta is Selena Pena and Juan Pena's daughter.
9. **C**
10. **C**

Set #8, page 25—Hurricanes

1. storms , Atlantic Ocean, Caribbean Sea, Gulf of Mexico—**subject**
2. hemisphere, hurricanes, direction, "eye"—**object of the preposition**
3. land, rain, winds, waves, buildings, homes, cars—**direct objects**
4. waves, *storm surge*—**subject**
5. Storm surges, reason, ocean, hurricane—**object of the preposition**
6. *meteorologist*, weather—**direct object**
7. Meteorologists, hurricanes, years—**subject**
8. Evidence, hurricanes, centuries—**subject**
9. word, "Hurakan", word,"hurricane"—**subject**
10. god, *Hurakan*, breath, water—**object of the preposition**

CHAPTER TWO: PRONOUNS

Set #1, page 32—Learning About Climate

1. her
2. she
3. he
4. us
5. He
6. We
7. they
8. She, us
9. she
10. they

Set #2, page 38—Learning About Butterflies

1. I; I
2. I; us
3. C
4. I; She
5. I; Who
6. C
7. I; I
8. I; We
9. I; me
10. C

Set #3, page 41—Pets

1. our
2. Her
3. My
4. Her
5. their
6. Our
7. Their
8. theirs
9. Your
10. Its

Set #4, page 45—A Trip to the Zoo

1. herself
2. ourselves
3. me
4. themselves
5. himself
6. themselves
7. myself
8. I
9. Myself
10. ourselves

Set #5, page 47—Spiders

1. Those
2. those
3. These
4. This
5. these
6. these
7. That
8. these
9. these
10. These

Set #6, page 52—Using Relative Pronouns

1. who
2. which
3. that
4. who
5. whom
6. who
7. which
8. whom
9. who
10. whom

Set #7, page 54—Using Interrogative Pronouns

1. which
2. Who
3. Whose
4. what
5. Who
6. What
7. Which
8. what
9. whom
10. What

Set #8, page 57—Using a Map

1. much
2. All
3. Many
4. anyone
5. something
6. Anyone
7. Both
8. both
9. anyone
10. someone

Set #9, page 60—Writing with Indefinite Pronouns

1. **I,** <u>Anybody</u> can write well if <u>he or she</u> works hard.
2. **I,** <u>Few</u> are in <u>their</u> rooms.
3. **I,** <u>Nobody</u> is done with <u>his or her</u> project.
4. **C**
5. **C**
6. **C**
7. **I,** <u>Someone</u> left <u>his or her</u> cake out in the rain.
8. **C**
9. **C**
10. **C**

CHAPTER THREE: VERBS

Set #1, page 66—Robots

1. attached
2. walk
3. roll
4. use
5. power
6. comes

Set #2, page 69—Early Presidents

1. George Washington was born in Virginia. **was PA**
2. Our second president was John Adams. **was PN**
3. Thomas Jefferson, our third president was the founder of the University of Virginia. **was PN**
4. Jefferson and Adams were lawyers. **were PN**
5. George Washington and Thomas Jefferson became famous. **became PA**
6. Both remain well respected. **remain PA**

Set #3, page 77—Confusing Verb Pairs

1. lie
2. set
3. sat
4. let
5. lie
6. set
7. lay
8. let
9. Set
10. sit

Set #4, page 82—Healthy Living

1. Participle
2. Participle
3. Infinitive
4. Gerund
5. Infinitive
6. Gerund
7. Gerund
8. Infinitive
9. Gerund
10. Infinitive

CHAPTER FOUR: MODIFIERS

Set #1, page 87—Sharks

1. twenty-five
2. Whale three hundred
3. Adult Great White twelve fourteen
4. adult Pygmy eleven
5. unusual
6. zero
7. hard
8. tough elastic
9. well-developed
10. one

Set #2, page 90—Using Often-used Common Adjectives

1. After everyone sat down, there were two empty seats left.
2. My little brother wants to go to school with me.
3. Alfredo is wearing a white shirt.
4. Has anyone seen my brown jacket?
5. Jorge's father is a kind man.
6. Maria has a small cut on her forehead.
7. I have lost an envelope full of important papers.
8. Clouds filled the blue sky.
9. José is being chased by a big dog.
10. Mateo wears a different jacket every day to school.

Set #3, page 92—More Commonly-used Adjectives

1. Carlos ate two green peppers.
2. Maria is honest and kind-hearted.
3. Katrina is carrying a little black purse.
4. Juan's father bought a new blue car.
5. Ugo can juggle three round, green balls.

6. The dirt is brown and cold.
7. Armando's computer is small and light.
8. Julio is creative and intelligent.
9. At the circus, we saw six black bears.
10. Alexis sent her grandmother three short letters.

Set #4, page 95—The Constitution of the United States

1. The Constitution created three independent branches of government that had **definite** responsibilities and had to work together if the government was to function.
2. Written in 1787, the Constitution is a **historic** document.
3. The United States was an **infant** country when the Constitution was written.
4. Writing the Constitution was a **hard** task.
5. At the time the Constitution was being written, the United States had an **inadequate** government.
6. The Framers wanted to meet and find a **fresh** way of running the country.
7. The **famous** meeting was called the Constitutional Convention.
8. The **initial** Constitution did not specifically mention personal rights.
9. Because the first ten amendments to the Constitution set our personal rights, these first ten amendments are **significant** amendments.
10. These **initial** amendments are called the Bill of Rights.

Set #5, page 98—Eagles

1. The
2. a
3. the
4. the
5. the
6. the
7. an, an
8. An
9. A
10. a

Set #6, page 101—Writing with Demonstrative Adjectives

1. This
2. Those
3. this
4. those
5. That
6. these
7. this
8. these
9. this
10. Those

Set #7, page 103—The First Americans

1. more	Their *migration* or journey probably first started over 11,000 years ago, and later many migrants followed.
2. all	Christopher Columbus first applied the name "Indian" to some Native Americans he encountered.
3. each	He believed that some islands he visited were part of the East Indies of Asia.
4. Many	Few tribes of Native Americans lived throughout North America.
5. Each	Some tribes had their special traditions and culture.
6. many	One of the few North American tribes is the Apaches.
7. most	As did some Native Americans, the Apaches believed that everything in nature had special powers.
8. Both	Other Apaches and the Navajos lived in the Southwest.
9. several	There were few Iroquois tribes.
10. few	All Iroquois tribes include the Mohawk, the Oneida, and the Seneca.

Set #8, page 105—Eating a Nutritious Breakfast

1. our breakfast
2. his breakfast
3. your body
4. his breakfast
5. his hunger
6. his experience
7. my energy
8. Your energy
9. our energy
10. Your breakfast

Set #9, page 107—Geekcorps: Bringing Technology to Everyone

1. very less
2. badly
3. usually
4. Typically recently
5. highly
6. completely
7. relatively rapidly
8. daily significantly
9. Currently extremely
10. nearly more

Set #10, page 111—Celebrations Around the World

1. popular
2. beautiful
3. unsuccessful
4. commonly
5. actual
6. literally
7. symbolically
8. excitedly
9. widely
10. widely

Set #11, page 114—A Day at the Beach

1. really
2. more
3. suddenly
4. hottest
5. brightly
6. careful
7. worse
8. higher
9. good
10. most

CHAPTER FIVE: PREPOSITIONS

Set #1, page 122 Using Compound Prepositions

1. next to
2. prior to
3. instead of
4. out of
5. in front of
6. in favor of
7. because of
8. similar to
9. instead of
10. next to

Set #2, page 124 George Washington as Our First President

1. in 1789
2. for two terms
3. for four years
4. until the year 1796
5. During his presidency, on December 15, 1791
6. over the years
7. to Mount Vernon, after his presidency
8. on a horseback ride, on December 12, 1799
9. during his ride
10. because of his ride, on December 14, 1799

Set #3, page 128 Polar Bears

1. in
2. like
3. over
4. under
5. of
6. to
7. around
8. on
9. off
10. on

Set #4, page 131 The Dangers of Smoking

1. <u>with reference to</u>
   There are many important facts *about* smoking.
2. <u>on the basis of</u>
   Each year, 390,000 Americans die *from* the effects of smoking.

3. <u>With reference to</u>
Concerning the risk of heart attacks, smokers have more than twice the risk.
4. <u>On the basis of</u>
From research, it is known that even smoking as few as one to four cigarettes a day can have serious health consequences.
5. <u>for the reason that</u>
Cigarette smoking is addictive *because* the nicotine in cigarette smoke causes an addiction.
6. <u>in order to</u>
The tobacco industry advertises *to* convince people that smoking is safe and glamorous.
7. <u>by reason of</u>
Most people begin smoking as teens *because* their friends are smoking.
8. <u>In order to</u>
To increase your chances of not smoking, avoid people who do.
9. <u>in excess of</u>
Smoking causes *more than* 80 percent of all lung cancers.
10. <u>On the basis of</u>
From all the scientific knowledge available, starting to smoke is one the worst decisions that you can make.

CHAPTER SIX: CONJUNCTIONS

Set #1, page 138—Earthquakes

1. We know earthquakes occur, **<u>but</u>** what causes them?
2. This shaking of the ground beneath our feet is usually not harmful, **<u>yet</u>** this shaking sometimes causes much property damage and deaths.
3. Scientists have studied what causes the rocks to release their energy, **<u>so</u>** they feel if they understand this, they might be able to predict where and when an earthquake will occur.
4. The shaking of the ground is caused by an abrupt shifting of rock along fracture lines within the planet Earth, **<u>and</u>** we refer these fracture lines as *faults*.

5. Scientists know that the rocks release their trapped energy when large sections of the Earth's rocky outer shell shift along a fault and breaks, **but** no one can accurately predict when this shifting will occur.
6. A hard outer crust covers the planet Earth, **yet** this crust is not solid, rather it is broken into massive rock pieces called *tectonic plates.*
7. The ground beneath our feet seems rock-solid, **but** a grid of slowly moving *tectonic plates* composes our planet's surface.
8. Most of this movement occurs along narrow zones between plates, **and** this is where the earthquakes occur.
9. The tectonic plates release great energy when they move, **yet** they move only at about the speed that your fingernails grow.
10. Sudden movement of the plates can release the energy trapped in the rock layers, **or** it can be released by a volcanic eruption, **or** manmade explosions can even release it.

Set #2, page 141—The Importance of Water

1. whether or
2. Not only but also
3. Although yet
4. not but
5. either or
6. Although yet
7. neither nor
8. either or
9. Whether or
10. Not only but also

Set #3, page 144—Fire Safety

1. Before
2. Once
3. Because
4. If
5. Unless
6. Although
7. Although
8. Once
9. If
10. Because

CHAPTER SEVEN: INTERJECTIONS

Set #1, page 150—The Ancient Olympics

1. Aha
2. Ah
3. Oh my
4. Goodness
5. Wow
6. Okay
7. Ah
8. Hooray
9. Oh
10. Hooray

CHAPTER EIGHT: SPELLING AND VOCABULARY

Set #1, page 158—Climate and Weather

1. ch**a**nge LVā ch**a**nges LVā h**a**ve SVă
2. st**a**te LVā **a**tmosphere SVă **a**t SVă **a** LVā pl**a**ce LVā
3. **a**tmospheric SVă g**a**ses SVă
4. **a**cid SVă r**ai**n LVā v**a**por LVā **a**tmosphere SVă
5. **A** LVā m**a**jor LVā volc**a**nic SVă m**ay** LVā **a**tmosphere SVă
6. ev**a**por**a**tion SVă, LVā precipit**a**tion LVā b**a**lance SVă
7. exp**a**nding SVă g**a**ses SVă p**a**th SVă **a** LVā fl**a**sh SVă
8. H**ai**l LVā **a**nd SVă p**a**ths SVă
9. hurric**a**nes LVā g**a**ther SVă cont**a**ct SVă
10. **a** LVā g**a**s SVă str**a**tosphere SVă radi**a**tion LVā

Set #2, page 160—California Explorers and Settlers

1. s**ea** LVē **e**xploration SVĕ Europ**ea**ns LVē t**e**chnological SVĕ dev**e**lopments SVĕ s**e**xtant SVĕ
2. Vásqu**e**z SVĕ l**e**d SVĕ Europ**ea**n LVē **e**xplorations SVĕ Am**e**rican SVĕ Southw**e**st SVĕ
3. Cort**e**z SVĕ l**e**d SVĕ **e**xpedition SVĕ **e**xplored SVĕ M**e**xico SVĕ
4. thr**ee** LVē v**e**ssel SVĕ Rodrígu**e**z SVĕ l**e**ft SVĕ w**e**st SVĕ M**e**xico SVĕ
5. Th**e** LVē **e**xpedition SVĕ fl**ee**t LVē Di**e**go SVĕ S**e**pt**e**mber SVĕ, SVĕ

6. Sebastian SVĕ European LVē explorers SVĕ reach LVē December SVĕ
7. went SVĕ next SVĕ tent SVĕ tree LVē
8. expedition SVĕ set SVĕ reached LVē
9. Mexico SVĕ people LVē encourage SVĕ settlers SVĕ
10. settlers SVĕ left SVĕ East LVē the LVē heading SVĕ

Set #3, page 162—Physical Properties of Matter

1. liquid SVĭ, SVĭ solid SVĭ
2. physical SVĭ, SVĭ is SVĭ anything SVĭ using SVĭ
3. everything SVĭ anything SVĭ
4. oxygen SVĭ still SVĭ liquid SVĭ, SVĭ why LVī is SVĭ
5. freezing SVĭ liquid SVĭ, SVĭ is SVĭ melting SVĭ in SVĭ its SVĭ solid SVĭ
6. ice LVī physical SVĭ, SVĭ
7. iron LVī chemical SVĭ occurring SVĭ period SVĭ time LVī
8. solid SVĭ grind LVī it SVĭ into SVĭ microscope LVī will SVĭ
9. diamond LVī is SVĭ crystal SVĭ lattice SVĭ which SVĭ organization SVĭ
10. liquids SVĭ, SVĭ in SVĭ between SVĭ positioned SVĭ solid SVĭ

Set #4, page 164—The Solar System

1. solar LVō objects SVŏ
2. not SVŏ own LVō
3. four LVō closest LVō
4. rocky SVŏ most SVŏ
5. only LVō known LVō
6. rotation LVō rotates LVō on SVŏ
7. holds LVō
8. solar LVō Pluto LVō
9. spots SVŏ known LVō sunspots SVŏ
10. Jovian LVō composed LVō rock SVŏ slow LVō solid SVŏ

Set #5, page 166—Properties of Metals

1. aluminum LVo͞o constitute LVo͞o
2. aluminum LVo͞o conductor SVŭ
3. spoon LVo͞o conducts SVŭ but SVŭ wooden LVo͞o
4. current SVŭ through LVo͞o
5. unstable SVŭ rusts SVŭ but SVŭ burns SVŭ
6. conductors SVŭ fused LVyo͞o
7. Fusible LVyo͞o fused LVyo͞o
8. Tungsten SVŭ fuses LVyo͞o
9. Aluminum LVo͞o pure LVyo͞o
10. Students LVo͞o aluminum LVo͞o

Set #6, page 168—The American Revolution

1. the Seven the severing the inconceivable
2. eventually the political and the colonists
3. Boston lawyer addressed the Superior and people
4. the resistance authority the colonies
5. father people degenerates tyrant and obedience
6. the and Indian the against the Austrians and the
7. William retirement and the the the the America
8. the the revenue the colonies
9. The the colonist
10. the Chancellor Exchequer convinced Parliament the colonists

Set #7, page 170—More About the American Revolution

1. Where /ər/ restore /ôr/ order /ôr/, /ər/
2. Later /ər/ year /îr/ massacre /îr/ learned /ûr/
3. schooner /ər/ burned /ûr/
4. December /ər/ their /âr/ later /ər/ speaker /ər/ hear /ûr/
5. port /ôr/ for /ôr/ harbor /ôr/ coercive /ûr/
6. toward /ôr/
7. their /âr/

8. **First** /ûr/ Carpent**ers** /ûr/
9. Th**ere** /âr/ th**ir**teen /ûr/ w**ere** /ûr/
10. b**ir**th /ûr/ f**ir**st /ûr/

Set #8, page 173—Spelling Correctly

1. Listen
2. knife
3. calf
4. treasure
5. answers
6. mnemonics
7. knee
8. Scissors
9. wrong
10. write

CHAPTER NINE: SENTENCE ENDINGS AND PAUSES

Set #1, page 187—Dental Health

1. ! exclamatory
2. . declarative
3. . declarative
4. ? interrogative
5. . declarative
6. . declarative
7. . declarative
8. . declarative
9. ? interrogative
10. ! imperative

Set #2, page 190—More About Dental Health

1. Pham asked, "Do you remember how we talked about bacteria forming plaque?"
2. "Plaque can cause cavities," I continued.
3. "The bacteria colony uses sugar for its food," replied Pham.
4. "The bacteria multiply faster when they have more sugar available to them," he said.
5. He said, "Some of the bacteria turn the sugar into a kind of glue."
6. "Once it forms, plaque is hard for us to remove," Pham said.
7. He also said, "It is the acid formed underneath the plaque that eats a hole in the enamel of our teeth."
8. "What should we do to keep plaque off our teeth?" I asked.
9. Pham said, "The dentist can use various techniques to remove the plaque and prevent cavities."
10. "I'm going to make a dental appointment today!" I exclaimed.

Set #3, page 194—Clara Barton—Founder of the American Red Cross

1. The Red Cross, a special group that helps people during disasters, is over 100 years old. appositive
2. Clara Barton is the founder of the American Red Cross, and she is champion of helping the less fortunate. simple sentences in a compound sentence
3. When she was eleven years old, her brother was seriously injured. introductory clause
4. While nursing him back to health, she learned much about medicine and helping sick and injured people. introductory clause
5. During the Civil War, Clara raised money for medical supplies and transported them herself to the front lines. introductory phrase
6. Because she gave so much care to the wounded soldiers, people began calling her the "Angel of the Battlefield." introductory clause
7. This hard work took a toll on her, and Clara became very sick. simple sentences in a compound sentence
8. To recover her health, she went to Switzerland and stayed with friends. introductory phrase
9. While she was in Switzerland, the founders of the International Red Cross asked her to start an American branch of the Red Cross. introductory clause
10. The American Red Cross began in 1881, and Clara Barton served as its first president for twenty-three years. simple sentences in a compound sentence

Set #4, page 199—Protecting Our Forests

1. Deforestation is caused by the following: clearing the trees away to provide land for agriculture, clearing the trees to create pasture land for cattle ranching, and clearing away trees to make room for roads and houses.
2. The consequences of deforestation are the following: global warming, soil erosion, and species extinction.

3. The *greenhouse effect* is a major cause of global warming, and the greenhouse effect results from increasing amounts of carbon dioxide being released into the atmosphere.
4. Forests act as a "carbon dioxide sponge" by absorbing the carbon dioxide from the atmosphere and using it to produce the carbon-based nutrients, such as carbohydrates, fats, and proteins that make up trees.
5. Unfortunately, when forests are cleared and the trees are either burnt or rot, these carbon-based nutrients are released as carbon dioxide.
6. Scientists believe that deforestation (the destruction of forests) contributes more than one-third of the carbon dioxide released into the atmosphere.
7. Many animals—more than half of the species on Earth—depend upon forests for food and shelter.
8. After the trees in a particular area have been removed, there is nothing to hold the soil in place.
9. As a result, areas experience widespread *erosion.*
10. This erosion is harmful for the following reasons: plants don't have enough soil for growth, the soil that has been eroded dumps into streams and kills the fish, and there is less soil to hold moisture.

CHAPTER TEN: WRITING SENTENCES

Set #1, page 205 Distinguishing Between Sentences and Sentence Fragments

1. Bonita and J.R. were looking forward to Gina's party. **S**
2. Roberto's father took him to the soccer game. **S**
3. Inside the box was a prize. **S**
4. On the side of the box. **F**
5. She gave me a pair of scissors. **S**
6. The scissors are on the desk. **S**
7. The large, red apple. **F**
8. It is I. **S**
9. The planets revolve around the sun. **S**
10. She hid behind the tree. **S**

Set #2, page 210—Protecting Yourself Against the Sun

1. types, are
2. Damage is
3. Exposure, causes
4. time, is
5. rays, are
6. sunscreen, protects
7. All, need
8. idea, is
9. People, are
10. people, are

Set #3, page 213—More About Protecting Yourself from the Sun

1. exclamatory
2. declarative
3. declarative
4. interrogative
5. declarative
6. interrogative
7. exclamatory
8. declarative
9. declarative
10. imperative

Set #4, page 215—Writing Simple Sentences

1. Juan is walking with his dog in the park.
2. Isis asked the police officer for directions to the stadium.
3. My new car is a red convertible.
4. Carlos scored a goal with one minute left in the match.
5. Please meet me in front of school.
6. Carla, what kind of music do you like?
7. It's hot today!
8. Linda, will you meet me at the mall?
9. What are you doing, Tom?
10. My favorite teacher is Ms. Garcia.

Set #5, page 218—Taking Care of Your Pet

1. compound
2. compound
3. simple
4. compound
5. simple
6. complex
7. simple
8. complex
9. compound-complex
10. complex

Set #6, page 220—More About Owning a Pet

1. Owning a pet is a lot of fun, but it is also a lot of work.
2. Because pets cannot take care of themselves, you must help with their care.
3. At least once a month, Luis gives his dog a bath, and he cleans out the doghouse.
4. Although you may be busy studying or doing other things, you should play with your pet every day.
5. While you are at school, your pet needs to have food to eat, and it also needs water to drink.
6. Since your dog cannot get its own food and water, you must make sure to provide food and water.
7. To make sure your pet is part of the family, you and the rest of your family must agree on rules for its behavior.
8. As soon as you bring it home, you should begin teaching your puppy or dog, and your other family members should also help train your puppy or dog.
9. While your dog might want it, never feed your dog chocolate candy, and never feed your dog anything with chocolate in it.
10. Since a dog cannot digest chocolate, it can kill it if it eats too much.

Set #7, page 225—Flowering Trees

1. **S**
2. **RO** If a tree is battered by a hurricane, **and** all of its leaves are stripped off, it may flower again although it is not spring.
3. **RO** During mild winters, trees flower early, **but** if snow and ice come after the flowers are out, the flowers will die.
4. **RO** When it warms up again, the trees may start growing leaves, **yet** they may not be able to produce fruit.
5. **S**
6. **S**
7. **S**
8. **RO** Some types have male and female flowers on the same tree; other types of trees have only female flowers or male flowers.

9. **RO** All trees have flowers, **and** it is the flowers that make the seeds.
10. **S**

CHAPTER ELEVEN: WRITING ESSAYS AND STORIES

Set #1, page 233—Taking Care of a Pet

Knowing what to feed your dog is very important to your dog's health. Because your dog depends upon you to feed it, it is up you to learn what it should eat. The best person to tell you this is your pet's veterinarian. Among other things, he or she will tell you that you shouldn't feed your pet table scraps because people food usually makes most dogs sick. Your veterinarian will also tell you that you should never feed chocolate to your dog. Chocolate is deadly to dogs! There is a lot of enjoyment from owning a dog, but there is also a lot of responsibility, especially when it comes to feeding your dog.

Set #2, page 238—City Mayors

I. The mayor of a large city is responsible for the executive and administrative duties in the city government.
   A. List a mayor's various duties.
   B. The mayor may not work at another job.

II. Citizens want a say in who will serve as their mayor.
   A. The residents elect their mayor through a citywide election.
   B. The mayor is elected to serve for a term of four years.
   C. Most cities allow a person to be a mayor for up to two terms.

Set #3, page 240—Writing an Essay

Topic: <u>Learning a New Language</u>

Thesis Statement: People who have mastered a second language will tell you that learning a new language is a lifetime challenge.

Outline:

I. Learning a new language is a lifetime challenge.
   A. Some students have unreasonable expectations.
   B. You need people and resources to help you.

II. Practice reading, writing, and speaking your new language every day.
   A. Use the library.
   B. Find fellow students and native speakers with whom to converse.

III. Work hard, but be patient with yourself.
   A. Your progress may be erratic.
   B. Learning a new language is worth the time and effort because it will lead to more opportunities and a better life.

Essay:

People who have mastered a second language will tell you that learning a new language is a lifetime challenge. Unfortunately, some students have unreasonable expectations about how long it will take them to become fluent speakers and proficient writers in their new language. In addition, some students limit their learning effort to the classroom. Those who have succeeded in learning a second language have asked for help from people, such as teachers, friends, and tutors, and used resources, such as books and instructional CDs to continuously improve their language skills.

To succeed at learning a new language, you should practice reading, writing, and speaking your new language every day, and this practice especially requires help from people and resources. One exceptionally good place for obtaining resources is your local public library. If you have a library card, you can check out books and instructional CDs for free. These free materials allow you to check out books and CDs at your current level of proficiency, and then, as your skills improve, you can return the previous material and check out more advanced materials. In addition, you should try to find fellow students and native speakers of your second language with whom to converse. You will be much more successful if you use these people and resources, along with your school classes, to work on learning your new language.

Work hard at learning your new language, but be patient with yourself. Your progress may be erratic. For a while, you may learn lots of new words and your speaking and writing will greatly improve, but then you may experience periods when it seems as if you are not improving. It's discouraging, yet normal. Don't panic, and certainly don't give up. If you are always working on improving your language skills, you will overcome the challenge of learning a new language. Learning a new language is worth the time, effort, and occasional frustration because it will lead to more opportunities and a better life.

INDEX